Ghosts of Athens
History and Haunting of Athens, Georgia

Tracy L. Adkins

Copyright © 2016-2018 by Tracy Adkins
All rights reserved.

ISBN-13: 978-1-5374987-9-9
ISBN-10: 1-5374987-9-7

First Printing, 2016
Second Printing, 2017

All photographs by the author
unless otherwise noted.

Printed in the U.S.A.

This book is dedicated to my parents, Anne and Bill,
who invested the time and effort to raise me well;
to my Sis, Stacey, who always supports me;
and to my Aunt Dotty and Uncle Mark
who left us too soon.

Contents

THE UNIVERSITY OF GEORGIA

Demosthenian Hall	3
The Wedding Cake House	17
Lustrat House	25
Candler Hall	31
The Stairway To Nowhere	35
Creswell Hall	43
Sigma Nu	49
Phi Mu	55
Sigma Phi Epsilon	61
Waddel Hall	65

HISTORIC ATHENS

The Morton Theatre	73
The T.R.R. Cobb House	89
Graduate Hotel	103
Fire Hall Number One	119
The Ware-Lyndon House	129
The Taylor-Grady House	139
Memorial Park	147
Old Athens Cemetery	155
Oconee Hill Cemetery	165
Arnocroft	175
Suntrust Bank	183
Bernstein Funeral Home	191

Contents

AROUND ATHENS AND NEARBY NEIGHBORHOODS

Athens-Ben Epps Airport	197
Lady Of The Blue Veil	201
The House On Glenhaven Avenue	209
The House On Milledge Circle	215
The Pope On Prince	221
Chappelle Gallery	227
Eagle Tavern	239

SMALL SPOOKS

The Barrow-Tate House	259
The John B. Cobb House	262
The Georgian Hotel	263
The Dancers	264
The Churchgoer	264
Delta Tau Delta	265
Uga Dance Building	266
The Mystery House On 78	267
Hargrett Rare Book And Manuscript Library	269

Acknowledgments

I extend my sincerest thanks to all those who shared their stories, knowledge, and enthusiasm that helped me compile the copious information required for this project, including the following:

Carol Bishop, Steven Brown, Gilbert Head, Elizabeth Elliott, Nicholas Twiner, Marla Whittington, John McKinney, Lucy Whitlock, Laura Deadwyler, Michael Southwick, Jeff Montgomery, Jeffery Clarke, Shannon Williams, Don Nelson, Sam Thomas, Kathy Chappelle, Alex Pershka, Maria Caudill, Monica Bischoff, Sandy Turner, Vanessa at the Athens Convention and Visitors Bureau, Amy Kissane, Evelyn Reece, Kathleen DeMarrais, Mrs. Zachmann at the Athens Fire Department Headquarters, Eric Frey, Janet Parker, Janine Duncan, Jason Flanagan and Stacey Mayes.

Introduction

I wrote this book for several reasons, but mostly because I wanted to read it.

When I travel, my hunt for a souvenir begins in a bookstore. I ask them if they carry a book that is a collection of local ghost stories. Usually they do! I enjoy them because ghost stories are more than just fascinating fun: you can learn a lot about the history of the area along the way.

I am happy to say that I now have bookshelves full of these spooky and historical collections. But, as my collection grew, I often wondered why my hometown, lovely Athens, Georgia, did not have a book of its own. I had heard rumors about the Wedding Cake House being haunted and stories about haunted frat houses. Didn't we have enough stories for a collection of our own?

It turns out, we do.

I decided I would compose the book that we were missing. And, once I started looking for Athens ghost stories, I found out that we have lots of them—much more than I ever realized. With the help of many librarians and historians, I began to bring together tales of haunted folklore that were in danger of being lost to the winds of time and document them in the context of history for all of us to enjoy. I also spoke with enthusiastic locals who are normal, regular folks, just like you and me, who wanted to share a tale of unusual events that they witnessed.

Claims of otherworldly interaction are nothing new. The concept of a ghost being a visible form of a deceased person dates back to the 14th century. Egyptian belief in the afterlife was compiled in *The Book of the Dead*. Even earlier, ghost stories can be found across all cultures and dating back to Mesopotamia.

Still, extraordinary claims require extraordinary evidence. And, many of the people I spoke to identified themselves as skeptics who never gave the paranormal a second thought...until it happened to them. While many strange events are easily explained away, others are not so simple.

All of this being said, I want to clarify a few things that this book is not: this book is not intended to convince anyone that ghosts exist. This book is not meant to be a comprehensive history of the city of Athens. While I have done research about the places and stories within, this book is not meant to be a comprehensive or authoritative anything at all.

This book is about one thing: storytelling.

The stories contained within have long been related among the people of Athens, in some cases, for many decades. And, it is in the telling of these stories to each other that people participate in a fun process that can potentially bring about a better understanding of community. At a minimum, perhaps an unexpected colorful thread is woven into the tapestry

Introduction

of someone's daily life. And, if a story is entertaining, perhaps that color will be passed on again and again.

So, whether you are a skeptic or a true believer or somewhere in between, my wish for you upon reading what I have written is to experience an unexpected smile, a nod of joy, a scoffing chuckle, and perhaps a twinkle of wide-eyed of wonderment along the way.

Some locations mentioned in this book are private. Please be respectful of current occupants.

THE UNIVERSITY OF GEORGIA

DEMOSTHENIAN HALL

The Demosthenian Literary Society was founded by the first graduating class of the Franklin College at the University of Georgia in February of 1803. It is the longest continuously running student organization in the country.

Demosthenian Hall was constructed in 1824 on North Campus very near the historic Arch at a cost of $4,000. It is a two-story, Federal style building and the fourth oldest building at the University of Georgia. Much of the original architecture has been maintained or restored, including hardwood floors, fireplace mantels, moldings, wainscoting, and unique ornate plasterwork.

In 1981, Demosthenian Hall underwent an extensive renovation. Prior to the renovation, the lower floor included one large room with a hallway and bathroom at the rear, as well as one long flight of stairs to the second floor. During renovations, walls were added in the lower chamber to create the library and President's office and the stairs were modified to include a landing halfway up. Albert Sams, the owner of the local Coca-

Cola bottling plant, donated museum quality furniture to complete the renovation.

The lower floor of Demosthenian Hall also now includes social space for members. The Upper Chamber is the meeting room of the Society. The unique plaster ceiling is one of few remaining original plaster ceilings from that era. The speaker's lectern has been dated to the 1820s and may have been built for the Hall. The entire upstairs has been almost completely restored to the original style, including wooden wainscoting and mantles.

Without question, one of the most famous members of the Demosthenian society is Robert Toombs. Toombs eventually served as a U.S. senator and as a general in the Confederate army, but his school days were more tumultuous than distinguished.

Toombs entered the University of Georgia in 1824 but, after constant fighting and antics, was dismissed a year later. After Toombs begged to be pardoned for his offenses, and his oratory skills gained him readmittance. However, his familiar rowdy behavior continued and the faculty dismissed him again in 1828 for chasing a citizen with a hatchet and a gun.

"When Bob Toombs was a student here, he pretty much got into trouble and stayed in trouble," declared University Archives Associate Gilbert Head, himself a Demosthenian Society member during school in 1975. "After being banished and reinstated, banished and reinstated, the straw that broke the camel's back was that Toombs used offensive language in a classroom setting and would not retract the language. Bob Toombs has had plenty to say, both inside and outside."

According to campus folklore, Toombs eventually took revenge for his repeated dismissals from the University. While commencement exercises took place in the campus chapel, Toombs stood under an oak tree outside and began a passionate speech. His speech drew the crowd away from the program and out of the chapel to listen. This was an insult to the University and testament to his abilities as an orator.

"Supposedly, the quality of his oratory was so stirring, it drew everybody out of the commencement ceremony," Mr. Head described. "At that time, there was a very large oak tree that stood on a little knoll where there is a sundial now. After his speech there, that tree became known as Toombs Oak. The tree was ultimately the victim of several lightning strikes, the last of which supposedly occurred as Toombs was on his deathbed breathing his last breath."

Today, Robert Toombs Oak is commemorated by a historical marker on North Campus and his portrait hangs over the fireplace in the upstairs meeting hall at Demosthenian Hall. A section of the Toombs Oak tree remains in the Upper Chamber and is held sacred by society members. Some members believe that Toombs' spirit remains in the tree and may be why he haunts the building.

"Upstairs is where his portrait hangs, where the stump from his oak tree stays, and where his spirit lives on in all members in the oration that takes place in the Hall. Every Thursday meeting carries on a 200-year tradition of incredible orators," said Nicholas Twiner, the currently elected Hall Administrator.

Many would also speculate that Toombs' spirit literally haunts the home of the literary society to this day. Mr. Twiner acknowledged that Demosthenian members joke about Toombs' ghost haunting the Hall or reference it casually. They even include the spook in society activities.

"If a meeting runs late into the night, a member will ask a question from Mr. Toombs' perspective," Twiner confided, "or, Bobby T., as he is affectionately known. Also, to become a member of the society, you have to get signatures. Sometimes, Bobby T. is allowed to sign."

By including him in proceedings, they hope to keep a healthy relationship with the late Mr. Toombs.

The society holds an annual election for officer positions. Before the election, candidates must stand on Toombs' stump in the Upper Chamber and give their stump speech. According to Mr. Twiner, "When standing on the stump, candidates hope to channel Mr. Toombs and be blessed with his gift of oration to help them win the election."

"It is interesting; most ghost stories are about one thing that happened one time that is an anomaly. The ghost of Robert Toombs at Demosthenian Hall is entrenched in our history as well as current daily activities," Mr. Twiner suggested. "We like to say he is a friendly ghost."

Every society member is given a key to the building and some members spend time in the Hall studying during the day or socializing at night. Since Robert Toombs' death, many members of the society have had strange experiences during time spent in Demosthenian Hall. Some members have heard footsteps and seen doors fly open. When the Hall is empty, phantom meetings have been heard. Unexplained cold spots are common. Sometimes thumping, dropping, or shaking sounds are heard when no source can be attributed to them.

"Over the summer, a student may sometimes stay at the Hall when they are between apartments," Mr. Twiner informed me. "One member was between apartments and sleeping downstairs in the Hall. Each night he was tormented by terrible nightmares. Finally, he could take it no more and he switched to sleep upstairs instead of downstairs.

"As of the first night they spent upstairs, the nightmares stopped. The member believes that he had the nightmares because Bobby T. was not happy that he was sleeping downstairs. He wanted the member to sleep upstairs in Bobby's predominant area of the building."

Gilbert Head recalled, "There are a lot of variations on the Robert Toombs ghost that have to do with carrying on in the wee small hours of the night up in the debate chambers upstairs only to be disrupted by a restless Robert Toombs who wants them to vacate or at least behave with a whole lot of decorum." He recalls reports of clanging noises and moaning.

"I remember one story that supposedly happened in the late sixties or early seventies to a couple that was fooling around in the debate chamber. The moaning the couple heard was severe enough during that late-night encounter for both of the participants to grab their clothes and take flight without bothering to get girded back up until they were out of the room. That story was still being told when I rejoined during graduate school in 2006."

Some versions of that story specify that when the couple looked up, the very ghost of Robert Toombs stood above them staring, causing them to bolt.

As told by Carol Bishop in her ghost tour, "Most of the members report hearing footsteps when no one else is around. Sometimes the footsteps are even accompanied by heavy breathing, as if someone has just finished a very intense run."

"In one instance, one of the lights in the hallway wouldn't turn off for three days, even when you continuously flicked the switch. Finally, someone said, 'Mr. Toombs, please turn off the light,' and the light switched off by itself."

Another story told relates that some members were upstairs in the debate chamber in the wee hours of the morning, around 1:30. They heard creaking and then footsteps on the stairwell. The students likened the sound they heard to what one would expect from Confederate army-issued boots. The footsteps came all the way up the stairs and continued into the middle of the debate chamber, but no one, person or ghost, was visible.

An alumnus Demosthenian member, whom I will call Mrs. B., described strange events from her time at Demosthenian Hall as well.

"This occurred during my junior year during the Fall of 2002. It was about 6:00 or 6:30 in the evening, twilight, but not fully dark. I was at Demosthenian Hall studying to kill time while I waited to meet a friend for a coffee date. I was alone.

"Sitting on the sofa on the back wall, I was reading when I became aware that I had been hearing a knocking sound for a while. The knocking sounds like it is coming from the bathroom and has a very regular cadence. After consideration, I decide that, although the building has sounds I commonly associate with it, I do not recall this knocking being one of the usual sounds. Trying to rationalize, I consider if it is possible that there are pipes or plumbing or anything that would be making the sound, but nothing seems plausible. I know what a knocking radiator sounds like, and this sound was definitely not that. This knocking was steady at 30 to 40 beats per minute.

"I finally thought, 'Oh, it's probably just acorns or something falling on the roof.' At this point, I am not freaked out.

"But, the longer I contemplated, it didn't make sense for acorns to fall at a regular rate. Especially since there was not an oak tree that overhung that corner of the building. So, I know it is weird, but I'm still not freaked out yet. And then, the sound moved.

"The regular cadence of the knocking continued, but it moved to the space underneath the stairs, which was right behind me. The knock, knock, knock now came directly from the other side of the wall where I sat.

"Again, I tried to rationalize. 'Maybe it is an animal stuck in the wall.' But, this made no sense for the regular, steady beat. I sat and listened to the knocking behind me, wondering.

"Finally becoming anxious, I moved to a chair closer to the front corner of the building. The sound moved also.

"Once again, the knocking comes from directly behind me.

Only this time, there is no space behind the wall situated directly behind me, because it is an external wall. The very noticeable, very regular knocking noise sounds like it is coming from inside the wall. Right behind me. That's when I just got the hell out of there.

"Something about this...whatever it was...didn't strike me as being Bobby T. I had spent plenty of time alone in the Hall late at night. I did a total library reorganization at one point and actually stayed overnight alone a couple of times. Then, I thought I had heard Bobby T. milling around upstairs in the debate chamber plenty of times.

"This time the sound was really different. Either Bobby T. was playing a prank on me or Demosthenian Hall has a second ghost. I just don't know."

It is worth mentioning here that one of the unusual qualities about the construction of Demosthenian Hall is that its exterior walls are stucco over brick construction and are two feet thick. How something could have been inside that solid wall to do any prankish knocking is a good trick, indeed.

Alumnus Demosthenian member Mr. C. recalls an incident from his time at the University:

"My first encounter happened during the Fall quarter of 1980, before the renovation. It was late one day and I was at the Hall by myself, studying. Dinner time was drawing near and I used the bathroom at the back. As I was drying my hands, I heard someone walk across the old tile floor and stop right outside the bathroom door. Within seconds, I opened the door expecting to see someone there. But, there was no one. I looked around but found no one else in the building.

"My second encounter occurred after the renovations had taken place. A group of us students were hanging out in the lower chamber when one of the new lampshades that had been donated by Mr. Sams started to move around by itself, as if someone had bumped into it. But, no one was close enough to the lamp to have bumped it. We were really shaken.

"The most creepy encounter I can relate happened on May 28, 1981. I remember the date because my first nephew was born that day. A group of students were hanging around the Hall until late. About 12:30 in the morning, we were exiting the rear door of the Hall when we heard what sounded like someone making noise inside. Since we thought we were the only ones there at the time, we immediately went back inside and searched both floors. We saw no one.

"Feeling apprehensive, we left again and piled into a car parked behind the Hall. As the car backed out, the light from the headlights crept up the back of the building. Someone in the car yelled, 'Look at that!' I looked up in time to see something in the window near the landing of the staircase. It looked like the lower part of a small person wearing dark pants. Another student in our group claimed to have seen a young man bend down to look out the window, then quickly run up the stairs. He appeared to be wearing a white shirt of 19th-century style. I didn't see a face, so maybe I saw him after he started running up the stairs.

Perhaps a former Demosthenian member from the 19th century has taken a permanent spot in the Hall, particularly in the rear hallway and stair area."

The following anecdotes are documented in the 1981 *Red and Black* newspaper article, "Strangers in the Night." Some of the statements seem to corroborate Mr. C.'s story.

"Ask Harry Knox, a junior in political science, and he'll tell you about one night last May. Knox was with two friends at Demosthenian Hall on North Campus around 1:30 a.m. talking. After leaving the Hall, Knox had to return to get something he had forgotten. As he was unlocking the rear door of the Hall, he heard something peculiar.

"It was as if I had startled someone and they ran up the stairs," Knox said. "It wasn't like a creak of the building."

After calling back both his friends, Knox searched the Hall, but found no one. No one had been hiding in the Hall or had entered the Hall while they had been there, Knox said.

After leaving the Hall a second time, Knox glanced back at a window located in the middle of the staircase. "It looked like someone was peering out of the window," he recalled.

"I could not see any features, Knox said, but he said he was sure about what he had seen.

Who, or what, has these people convinced the Hall is haunted? The general consensus seems to be it's the ghost of Robert Toombs.

Many Demosthenians, including Jim Ellington, a sophomore in political science, claim to have had many encounters with Toombs. Around midnight of one night last May, Ellington was with a friend in the upper chamber looking at some of the artifacts that line the walls. No one else was in the Hall.

Suddenly, they heard something walking down the aisle between the rows of chairs that fill the chamber. The footsteps stopped at the speaking lectern and Ellington and his friend quickly exited.

Ellington was also seated downstairs at 1:00 a.m. last year speaking with a couple of friends when a lampshade started twirling.

"It did it of its own volition," Ellington said. Ellington said they tried to recreate the twirling, but failed. "We couldn't think of any practical explanation," he said.

Other tales of similar incidents abound. People hear footsteps and doors flying open. At times, it has been no more than a feeling that someone or something was there. "At times, we have felt a presence," Ellington said.

Doug Craig, a sophomore political science major, was alone in the Hall around 5:30 p.m. last year. He went to wash his hands in a bathroom located near the rear of the Hall, when he heard footsteps.

"It was hard-soled shoes," Craig said. He couldn't tell from which direction they came, but they stopped at the back door and then he heard a peculiar sound. "A heavy, heavy sigh, a moan sigh," Craig said. "As if someone had just walked a mile."

Craig thought it was a prank and stepped out to see, but no one was there. "I still have cold chills thinking about it," Craig said.

Demosthenians have different ideas about why Toombs should remain to haunt the Hall, but Knox may have the best.

"I know that Robert Toombs was a cantankerous character in life; why shouldn't he be a cantankerous character in death?" Knox said. "Why shouldn't he haunt a Hall?"

Ellington feels that the ghost is benevolent. "Not to sound trite about it. The ghost does not scare me. It's a friendly ghost," he said.

Craig also said he didn't think the ghost was a prankster.

"I tend to think it's not a poltergeist," he said.

Toombs has changed some views on ghosts. "I tend to believe they exist now," Ellington said. "Until you've experienced it, you kinda chuckle about it and dismiss it."

The strange goings-on at the Hall have ceased according to Ellington, and nothing has happened since last May. Nothing will probably happen either for those going ghost hunting, he said.

"If you came up here expecting something, nothing would happen," Ellington said.

However, Knox feels that they haven't heard the last of Toombs. "Oh, no. I think he's waiting on a good opportunity."

Mr. Twiner noted that in addition to its central use by members, Demosthenian Hall is used for events such as receptions for University events and as a dressing area for weddings at the University Chapel next door. Perhaps Toombs will select such an event to be the opportunity he has waited for to make his presence known yet again.

Demosthenian Hall

Robert Toombs portrait in the debate chamber

Stump from Toombs Oak

Demosthenian Hall References

Bishop, Carol. "Haunted North Campus Walking Tour Script." Athens-Clarke Heritage Foundation tour on July 20, 2010.

"Ghosts (from page 1)" (Unidentified clipping from the Georgia Ghosts folder in the Hargrett Library collection.)

Head, Matthew. "Ghosts of Athens, GA (Long but Good!)." *Google Groups*. Newsgroup post. 3 May 1999.

Helms, Greg. "Strangers in the night: Demosthenians are haunted year round by the ghost of Robert Toombs." *The Red and Black*. October 30, 1981.

Mcafee, Marc. "VIDEO: North Campus Ghost Tour." *The Red and Black*. 22 Oct. 2009. Web. 04 Sept. 2016.

Wikipedia contributors. "Demosthenian Literary Society." *Wikipedia, The Free Encyclopedia*. 5 Sep. 2016. Web. 5 Sep. 2016.

Author interview with Gilbert Head, Archival Associate for the University Archives at the University of Georgia

Author interview with Nicholas Twiner

[Letter from Mr. C. via Nicholas Twiner]

[Letter from Ms. B. via Nicholas Twiner]

THE WEDDING CAKE HOUSE

Many visitors to Athens pass by a remarkable historic home at the corner of Milledge and Baxter streets. The Alpha Gamma Delta house, also known as the Thomas-Carithers house, is located at 530 South Milledge Avenue. It was originally built as a private home in 1896 by William Winstead Thomas, an accomplished local architect and engineer. It is true Beaux Arts Classicism, complete with stained glass windows and Tiffany beveled-glass doors.

The home was later bought by James Yancey Carithers as a wedding gift for his daughter, Susie. In fact, the wedding-cake like appearance of the exuberant, white, storied home gave rise to the building's well-known nickname: the Wedding Cake House.

When the day of Susie's wedding arrived, she walked on a cloud and daydreamed about her impending wedded bliss. But, that dream was fated not to come true. The hour of the wedding arrived but poor Susie's betrothed did not.

Susie waited. Guests waited. After hours passed, Susie was finally resigned to having been jilted at the altar.

Grief-stricken and not wanting to see the pitying looks of departing guests, Susie fled, unnoticed, to the attic of the home. Alone in the attic just above the honeymoon suite, she hanged herself.

Later, the full extent of the tragedy revealed itself when her groom did arrive, having only been delayed by a carriage accident on his way to the ceremony.

In 1939, the Alpha Gamma Delta sorority purchased the Wedding Cake House from James Carithers' widow and they began using it as chapter housing. The home was listed on the National Register of Historic Places on Jan. 8, 1991 and was renovated in 2013.

Through the years that sorority sisters made their home there, when they experienced odd occurrences, "Susie" was often to blame. The girls theorize that Susie is trapped in time by tragedy and now makes periodic appearances in the home.

"It's a story that everyone in this sorority is very familiar with," said former AGD member Linda Lewis. "She's a very friendly ghost." Ms. Lewis said that she has never seen or heard anything out of the ordinary while in the house. She added, "But, when the girls are away for a weekend and you're here alone, the house does get spooky." (Sanderlin)

One anonymous AGD member insisted several members have seen the ghost. "There are two rooms under the attic where she hanged herself. I lived in one." she said. "I thought I heard her," the woman says. "I did hear a lot of noises from the attic." Susie was described as having dark hair and wearing a white gown. "One of the girls in the next room said she saw her." Susie is reported to have appeared once only from the waist up. According to one former AGD President, the members all avoid the attic. "We don't go up there very often and never alone." They try to keep the attic door closed, but keeping it shut has been a problem. Despite being difficult to move, the large door tends to open itself after it has been closed. (Coffee)

AGD member Nancy Crist, who occupied the room where Susie was to be married, claimed to have seen the ghost many times. She claimed to see Susie dressed in a filmy white gown standing inside a door which had been securely locked. Around midnight one evening, Nancy awoke to see her door open and close repeatedly. She investigated for a logical cause for the event, but found no one, mortal or otherwise, anywhere near the door or in the hallway. Apparently, Susie had more tricks up her sleeve. Later that night, something unseen lifted up the sheet off Nancy's roommate as she slept. Other AGD members reported doors opening mysteriously, objects about their rooms missing or moved from their place. (Peeples)

The Red and Black article "Sorority house haunted by heartbroken bride" describes members' experiences:

> "I personally have never seen the ghost, but I know a lot of girls who have," said Amanda Ellis, a sophomore from Lake Arrowhead, Calif., who lived in the house in 2003.
>
> Some report that faucets have started running on their own, lights have turned on and off by themselves, doors have swung open without anyone near them and faces have appeared in windows.
>
> "The door to my bedroom and my roommate's closet door randomly swing open on their own," said Sarah Reiser, a sophomore from Winchester, Va.

One sister is sure that most members are convinced of Susie's presence. But, they consider Susie as a protective big sister rather than a menace to be feared. Susie has not harmed anyone, but she has startled many. Sometimes she makes her presence known with faint weeping sounds or by making the lights blink.

The 1989 article "Meet Suzie the sorority ghost" by Allison Smrekar details the following:

> Pam Mosely, a sophomore journalism major and current engagement suite resident, said a few odd coincidences in the room have led her to believe the legend. "Last quarter we were changing a light bulb, and just as we finished changing one, a different one blew up — not just went out, but blew up," she said. "It happened three times in a row with different bulbs," Mosely said. "It was probably the wiring, but when we checked, everything seemed fine."
>
> Jennifer Ellis, a sophomore political science major, and Jennifer Smentek, a senior English major, live in the VIP suite, the room which supposedly belonged to Susie. Smentek said they've also had uncanny experiences there. "One evening Jennifer Ellis was in the house by herself, and she said she heard something that distinctively sounded like a woman weeping," Smentek said. "She said it seemed like it was coming from one corner of the room. The next night, I was in the house when no one else was there, and when the air conditioner cut off, I could have sworn I heard the same thing." I may have been hearing things, because she said something about it, but there are other weird things, like lights flickering and an old painting on the staircase that gives you the feeling of a presence when you walk past," she said. "It's just eerie little things nobody is afraid of that just make us wonder," Smentek said.

More recent experiences were also described in a 2012 article:

> AGD members have reported a number of strange occurrences including unexplained noises, shadowy figures, and objects that move by themselves.
>
> In 2004, a student filming a story about the haunted home recorded a framed photo tumbling from a bookshelf. Sorority sisters also report doors opening and closing on their own, faucets turning on and off, the sound of a chair moving in the attic, and lights flickering with no explanation. The antique piano in the parlor has also been known to play by itself, its rusty, discordant notes echoing throughout the home. Some girls report seeing faces in windows, while others have seen a wispy figure in their bedroom.
>
> "Every year she's supposed to come through the windows to commemorate her death," resident Shae Virtue said in the 2004 video report. "She walks through the panes, walks through the room, opens our door, and then walks back up to the attic."

In her article "The Alpha Gamma Delta Ghost," recent AGD member Danielle Profita shared some of her experiences:

> The first time I experienced Susie was in August, when I was walking through the hallway back to Engagement around 9 o'clock at night. There was a huge rumbling coming from the attic and I could feel it in the walls as I walked into our room, which incidentally is right next to the eerie stairway to the attic. On a previous venture up to the attic with my roommates I had seen that there were about 60 old, wooden chairs there but, oddly enough, there are just beams above our room.
>
> I had heard stories of Susie moving things around in the attic but I never knew it would make such a ruckus.

Nevertheless, this was only the beginning. Everyday [when] I walk in and out of our room, I look up the stairway to the attic to see if Susie is there. Boy, is that an eerie staircase with an even eerier 4-foot-tall door. In Engagement, we've seen hangers fall off hooks and out of closets, doors and closets opening unexpectedly, locks getting stuck and artwork falling off walls. When these things happen, we usually get small knots in our stomachs for a hot minute and then immediately laugh it off, thanking Suz for the visit. Even though we are technically the "special" room, Susie has visited pretty much every room in the old part, including downstairs. In the TV room, I've seen the mini chandeliers swing and flicker, in the Music Room the piano has been heard in the dark and in the Gentleman's Parlor, the doors have opened unexpectedly.

All in all, we all have our Susie days, but most of the time we are just living in a house that is 119 years old.

Stories about these events can be found in copious sources, but the information is often conflicting. According to some genealogical records, James Carithers had no children. Newspaper accounts of a missing groom or suicidal bride cannot be found. Alternate versions of the tale say Susie was the daughter of William Winston Thomas, not James Carithers, but William's daughters were named Gertrude and Isabel. Regardless of inconsistencies, the story persists as one of Athens' longest running legends.

The Wedding Cake House
References

Coffee, Hoyt. "Spirits still roam Athens." *The Red and Black*. October 28, 1983. (Clipping from the Georgia Ghosts folder in the Hargrett Library collection.)

Davis, Melissa. "Ghosts Among the Kudzu." *DigitalCommons@Kennesaw State University*. Kennesaw State University, Web.

Ferguson, Anna. "Sorority House Haunted by Heartbroken Bride." *The Red and Black*. 24 Oct. 2003. Web. 09 Sept. 2016.

Head, Matthew. "Ghosts of Athens, GA (Long but Good!)." *Google Groups*. Newsgroup post. 3 May 1999.

Peeples, Gayle. "Ghost Story." *Georgia Impression*. Vol 7 Number 1. (Undated clipping from the Georgia Ghosts folder in the Hargrett Library collection.)

Morgan, Terry. "Athens has its share of ghastly ghouls and Halloween horrors." *The Red and Black*. (Undated clipping from the Georgia Ghosts folder in the Hargrett Library collection.)

Profita, Danielle. "The Alpha Gamma Delta Ghost." Odyssey. *Theodysseyonline.com*. 16 Feb. 2015. Web. 09 Sept. 2016.

Sanderlin, Phil. "The haunting: Several Athens houses have legends of ghosts and noises in the night." *The Athens Observer*. October 30, 1980. (Clipping from the Georgia Ghosts folder in the Hargrett Library collection.)

Shah, Mira. "Sorority spook: A ghost in AGD." *The Red and Black*. April 25, 1991. (Clipping from the Georgia Ghosts folder in the Hargrett Library collection.)

Smrekar, Allison. "Meet Suzie the sorority ghost." *The Red and Black*. March 15, 1989. (Clipping from the Georgia Ghosts folder in the Hargrett Library collection.)

"Sorority House Ghost Helps Others Find Love." *Ghostsnghouls.com*. 12 Apr. 2012. Web.

The Athens-Clarke Heritage Foundation Walking Tour. http://www.athenswelcomecenter.com/images/milledge_ave_walking_tour.pdf

LUSTRAT HOUSE

The Lustrat House on the North Campus of the University of Georgia is located at 230 South Jackson Street. Built in 1847, Lustrat House is the seventh-oldest building on campus. The house served as campus housing for University faculty so that teachers in residence could monitor students. Lustrat is the only remaining faculty house on North Campus.

A number of University employees have had the good fortune to call the Lustrat House their home. This occupancy history is described by Larry Dendy in *Through the Arch: An Illustrated Guide to the University of Georgia Campus*:

> The first occupant was John LeConte, a professor of natural history. Charles Morris, an English professor and former Major in the Confederate army, and his family lived here in the early 1880s. The last occupant was Joseph Lustrat, who lived in the house from 1897 until he died in 1927. A native of France, Lustrat came to UGA with a law degree from the Sorbonne, but spent thirty years teaching languages. The building served for a

time as a house museum for paintings and furnishings owned by Ilah Dunlap Little, benefactor of UGA's main library, and for several years it was the office of the University president.

Lustrat House is named for its last faculty occupant, Joseph Lustrat, the head of the Department of Romance Languages.

Lustrat House was originally constructed on a site further north than its present location. In 1905, when the construction of a new University library was underway, the home was occupied by Dr. Morris who argued against the plan to move the building. When the house was moved to the current location against his wishes, Dr. Morris refused to move with the home and quit the University as a result of the dispute.

This was difficult for Dr. Morris, who was known to enjoy his time in the home, sitting in his rocking chair by a warm, roaring fire in the fireplace of the front room. Apparently, Dr. Morris eventually gave in and did relocate with the home to its new location. It just happens that he did so after his demise.

During the time the Lustrat family occupied the home, Marie Lustrat claimed that on cold winter nights, the ghost of Dr. Morris would return. The family repeatedly saw the ghost of Dr. Morris seated in the dining room at a desk near the window.

Footsteps are heard in empty dark rooms. Sometimes, a mist appears and takes the shape of a tall man in a Confederate army uniform who moves toward the front room. Then, as members of the Lustrat family have claimed, Dr. Morris is seen sitting in his favorite chair by the fire, rocking quietly in the night, back and forth. Sometimes the chair rocks all night with no occupant seen sitting in it.

In more recent years, some have claimed to see a figure in uniform standing in a window of the Lustrat house. It is suggested that the specter, often called "the Admiral," could be Professor Charbonnier, who lived at the residence until his retirement in 1897. But, it could also be Dr. Morris revisiting his military service days in Virginia as a Confederate officer.

During the 1970s, when it was used for storage, the home underwent renovations and the fireplaces were bricked up and plastered over. Afterward, the sightings of Dr. Morris diminished. Perhaps Morris was frustrated by the closed-up state of his beloved fireplaces.

In later years, the building housed the offices of University President Fred Davison who served as the University president from 1967-86. He had the third-longest tenure among UGA presidents and died at 74 years old. During that time, Dr. Morris' favorite sitting room was used as a conference room. Some theorize that "the long, dry discussions of University policy have driven the old Confederate soldier away." (Sanderlin)

Mrs. Connie T. Penley, secretary to President Davison, smiled when she was told about the old legend. "We haven't seen the ghost," she said. "And we haven't heard any footsteps, not in all the years we've been here." (Sanderlin)

The Lustrat House is currently the home to the University of Georgia's Office of Legal Affairs. If anyone has recently seen Dr. Morris, they are keeping mum about it. Perhaps Dr. Morris has indeed vacated his beloved home, or perhaps no one is brave enough to speak out about the unexplained. Perhaps someone will replace the rocker in the sitting room, sit back, and see what happens.

Lustrat House

Lustrat House
References

Belcher, C.W. "Will the Ghost Walk Again? Lustrat House Stirring." *Athens Daily News.* October 31, 1968. (Clipping from the Georgia Ghosts folder in the Hargrett Library collection.)

French, Jana. "Haunted Places on Campus." *The Red and Black.* 09 Jan. 2015. Web. 09 Sept. 2016.

Head, Matthew. "Ghosts of Athens, GA (Long but Good!)." *Google Groups.* Newsgroup post. 3 May 1999.

Davis, Melissa. "Ghosts Among the Kudzu." *DigitalCommons@Kennesaw State University.* Kennesaw State University. Web.

Dendy, Larry. "Lustrat House." *Through the Arch: An Illustrated Guide to the University of Georgia Campus.* Chapter Two. 40. Print.

Sanderlin, Phil. "The haunting: Several Athens houses have legends of ghosts and noises in the night." *The Athens Observer.* October 30, 1980. (Clipping from the Georgia Ghosts folder in the Hargrett Library collection.)

Thompson, Jim. "Ex-UGA President Dies." *Onlineathens.com. Athens Banner-Herald.* 29 Apr. 2004. Web.

Athens Folklore email from the Georgia Ghosts folder in the Hargrett Library collection.

"The University of Georgia's Lustrat House is haunted!" (Unidentified clipping from the Georgia Ghosts folder in the Hargrett Library collection.)

CANDLER HALL

In 1900, the only two dormitories at the University of Georgia, Old College and New College, were full to capacity, so the Georgia Legislature approved $45,000 to build a new one. Construction began on June 14, 1901, and residents moved in during January of 1902. The new building located at the north end of Herty Field was named Candler Hall in honor of Governor Allen Daniel Candler.

The design of Candler Hall included columns on the front of the building which drew comparisons to Buckingham Palace. Soon after, the boys living there referred to themselves as the "Barons of Buckingham."

Residents of the three dorms developed heated rivalries on intramural sports teams, which resulted in fistfights, broken windows and banisters, and animals being turned loose in the buildings. In 1926, when Candler Hall housed freshmen boys, they notoriously tangled with the sophomores of New College. One sophomore had visited a downtown movie theater and stolen a poster of actress Myrna Loy. He hung the trophy at New College. Soon, the poster disappeared and then reappeared posted at Candler Hall.

The ensuing fracas resulted in Chancellor Charles Snelling being accidentally doused in ammonia as he intervened to stop the fight. In the end, every window was broken out at Candler Hall, but the Myrna Loy poster remained.

The Barons of Buckingham were displaced in 1918 when Candler Hall served as an infirmary during the Spanish Flu Epidemic. In March of 1942, Candler Hall was renovated for use by the U.S. Navy's Pre-Flight School and renamed Yorktown Barracks by the Navy. The dorm was returned to the University in 1943, the same year that female students began being housed in the dorm.

One sailor who was stationed in the naval hospital on Lumpkin Street had trouble letting go of his Candler Hall digs. At seven o'clock each morning, he stood outside the dorm and shouted for the girls to wake up. After several days of these antics, the girls retaliated by throwing oranges, water, and shoes at him while he yelled. Not discouraged, the sailor changed tactics. For his morning visit, he subsequently rode a motorcycle around the building in the hopes he would be a harder target to hit.

Today, none of the window panes in Candler are original. The 1926 Myrna Loy battle destroyed the first-floor windows. Others were demolished due to a resident who was building a bomb that went off. The remaining windows were finished off by overzealous students who exploded a barrel full of gasoline at Herty Field while celebrating the University of Georgia's winning the Southern Intercollegiate Athletic Association championship in baseball in 1911.

In 1953, Candler Hall was in dire need of repairs. It was closed and seemed destined for the wrecking ball until University President O.C. Aderhold decided to save it. After renovations, new office spaces in Candler Hall housed the Department of Student Activities, the Pandora yearbook, the University Chaplain, and the Anthropology Department. In 1956, it was converted back into a dormitory.

The Winter quarter of 1966 was the last time Candler Hall was used for student housing. Afterward, it was converted back to offices.

Renovations in 2003 restored many original features that had been removed over the years, such as its hardwood floors and ten-foot ceilings, and stairwells were relocated to their original locations. Candler Hall now houses the Department of International Affairs.

During the time that Candler Hall was a dormitory, it had a somewhat creepy reputation. There were students who reported waking from sleep and becoming aware of a presence in the room with them. They claimed that it felt as if someone was standing beside their bed and leaning over them.

The stairwell was notorious. One student reported having the sensation of passing someone in the stairwell, although they could plainly see that no one was there. Then, he heard the sound of chains being dragged up the stairs.

Perhaps the Candler Hall chain-dragger is not always invisible, though. As told by Carol Bishop in her ghost tour:

> A common trick was to encourage unsuspecting newcomers to the campus to play a game of bridge in Room 13. That's because a ghost with an affinity for bridge was said to occasionally stop by that room. More than once, it was reported that the apparition of a male figure holding a dagger appeared above men playing a game of bridge in that room.
>
> In one instance, the specter was even seen outside Room 13 on the stairway. A student was sitting on the stairs with his nose stuck in book studying for a test. The young man felt a breeze and heard the clanking sound of metal. He looked up to the see

a hazy figure staring down at him pointing a dagger toward his face. His friends found the poor student passed out and thought he was dead. Thankfully he was revived and was able to recount his strange tale.

A portrait was allegedly found—unearthed during one of the building's many renovations. Some claimed the portrait was of a young man who hanged himself while living there and whose restless spirit still walked the hallways. The painting was eventually turned over to the Georgia Museum of Art.

On the evening of November 5, 1905, University senior William Samuel Loyd was in his first-floor dorm room playing with a gun when it discharged accidentally. After being struck in the abdomen by the bullet, he died from blood loss within an hour. Perhaps he is the one who leaned over students as they slept, tragically doomed to seek help for a wound that will never heal.

As Candler Hall has existed for well over one hundred years, many souls have passed through its corridors. More than one may never have left.

Candler Hall
References

CANDLER HALL. http://intl.uga.edu/about/candler. Web. Accessed 09 August. 2016.

Head, Matthew. "Ghosts of Athens, GA (Long but Good!)." *Google Groups*. Newsgroup post. 3 May 1999.

School of Public & International Affairs. UGA'S BUCKINGHAM PALACE. http://spia.uga.edu/about/facts. Web. Accessed 09 August. 2016.

THE STAIRWAY TO NOWHERE

Joseph Emerson Brown, often referred to as Joe Brown, was born on April 15, 1821, in South Carolina and moved to Union County, Georgia at a young age. In 1840, Brown sought further education and drove a yoke of oxen 125 miles to Anderson, South Carolina, where he exchanged the oxen for eight months' board and lodging.

Politics was in Brown's blood. In 1849, he was elected to the Georgia State Senate and was the 42nd Governor of Georgia from 1857 to 1865.

After the fall of Atlanta, Union General Sherman began his March to the Sea, from Atlanta to Savannah, with Georgia's state capital, Milledgeville, in his path. As Northern troops closed in and the fall of Milledgeville was imminent, Governor Brown attempted to remove important state records. Failing to find any other men up to the task in the midst of the chaos, Brown went to the penitentiary and offered a pardon to each convict who would help load the train with state property. Afterward, each one was given a suit of gray and a gun, and they were formed into a military company.

In 1864, Brown called for an end to the war and was briefly held in Washington, D.C., as a political prisoner. The Confederacy collapsed in April 1865.

Brown was the Chief Justice of the Supreme Court of Georgia from 1865 to 1870 and then resigned to become president of the Western and Atlantic Railroad. Politics drew him back in when was elected to the U.S. Senate in 1880 and became the first Georgia official to support public education for all children. He finally retired in 1891 due to poor health.

Joseph Brown died on November 30, 1894, but he was memorialized in several ways. Margaret Mitchell's blockbuster novel, *Gone with the Wind*, made references to Governor Brown. And in 1932, Joseph E. Brown Hall was completed on the campus of the University of Georgia and named in his honor.

In contemporary times, Joe Brown Hall is less likely to conjure images of Confederate-era glory than inspire hushed whispers about a mystery and a strange stairwell. It was the location of an incident during the 1970s that haunts University of Georgia students to this day.

Most people understand the legend of Joe Brown Hall to be about a suicide that dates back to the 1970s, when the building was a dormitory. The story that circulates reports that, as students were leaving the dorm to head home for Christmas break, one student remained behind. For reasons known only to himself, the student supposedly committed suicide by hanging himself in his upper-floor dorm room.

A tragic story becomes bleaker as the body of the student goes undiscovered for the entirety of the holiday break.

As the other students returned to the dorm, an incredibly foul odor greeted them. Eventually a janitor and a resident assistant discovered the poor lad's body, bloated and leaking bodily fluids. One student at the time told a newspaper that "it didn't even look human."

Gilbert Head, Archival Associate for the University Archives at the University of Georgia, was a student at the University in 1975 and remembers those events well. "I came here in 1975, so the incident was still fairly fresh. People were still talking about it."

Head revealed information about the case that is not commonly part of the well-known legend: "This was a case of auto-erotic asphyxiation. The gentleman engaged in this just as everyone was going their separate ways at Thanksgiving. He had tied a tie or a belt around his neck and the doorknob of the closet. And that's where they found his body when the students came back after the long break. Fortunately, it was cold because, even though the smell was bad, it's nowhere near as bad as it could have been had it been later in the year."

Despite several thorough cleanings, the horrible stench of death returned again and again to the dorm room where the tragedy occurred. Bloodstains in the dorm room reappeared no matter how many times they were scrubbed. The cleaners for the building grew frustrated and unnerved, both by the recurring horrible smell and by strange occurrences that began to plague the crew who worked at night. After hearing unexplained creepy noises numerous times, no one wanted to be in the building after sunset and the workers eventually refused to work there at night. Similarly, students who occupied the dorm room after the event reported hearing noises.

To appease the cleaning crew and make better use of a space no one wanted to live in, the building was remodeled and the creepy dorm room at the top of the stairs was sealed off. Carol Bishop of the University Archives has investigated the area. "If you knock on the wall, it's obviously hollow where they closed up the room."

One architectural quirk resulted from the dorm remodel. When they closed off that section of the building, the stairwell that formerly led to the room now led up a few steps and ended in a wall. This area quickly gained the reputation as "The Stairway to Nowhere."

The remodel did not put an end to the problems in the building. Even after it was closed off, people working in the building would hear strange noises behind the new wall. Some claimed to hear sounds of knocking coming from the sealed room.

Associate Professor of Comparative Literature Dezso Benedek spoke to *The Red and Black* newspaper: "I heard knocking noises myself coming from the walls," he said.

Some have claimed to see a face looking in the windows of the building at night. Chris O'Neal, a junior from Scarborough, Britain, said, "My friends and I went over there yesterday. The door that leads to that stairwell was slightly ajar," he said. "When I went to open it, it snapped shut."

"I've been told that some kind of spirit houses within the wall," said Martin Kagel, a professor and Germanic & Slavic Studies department head. "I'm not very superstitious but I do work late nights, often around midnight," Kagel said. "It does get awfully quiet. Let's just say I wouldn't rule it out."

Additionally, some people supposedly have problems with mirrors in that space that show strange or no reflections.

No one is sure exactly who did it, but someone who was tired of the kerfuffle hung a poster on the wall in the place where the stairs ended abruptly. The poster is the size of a door and the image is a series of doorways that repeat into the distance. The effect is that instead of looking like a stairway that ends in a blank wall, it appears to be a stairway that leads to a hallway with many doors. Some theorize the image is an enlarged photograph of the apartment of German writer Johann Wolfgang von Goethe.

Rumors say this was done to make the spot less creepy since it no longer looked like a stairway to nowhere. Others hope that the illusion might encourage a ghost to see the "hallway" as a route for escape so it could exit to an appropriate plane of existence and stop bothering occupants in the building.

Carol Bishop is aware of the notoriety of the infamous poster in the Stairwell to Nowhere. "It's still there. It's quite famous," she said. All the more reason for Bishop to include the location when she led a Ghost Walk tour for the Athens-Clarke Heritage Foundation. "Occasionally someone catches a fleeting glimpse of a young man standing at the top of the stairs. This is also where a cold spot can often be felt," she says.

Gilbert Head is skeptical about the source of the cold spot. "It's not so much a ghost as it is environmental anomalies," he said. "Parapsychological researchers have actually gone over there and put a thermometer on it and there's a cold spot there that registers approximately where the gentleman's dorm room had been."

If you find yourself inside Joe Brown Hall, be aware of your surroundings. Not every door and stairwell is what it seems to be.

The Stairway to Nowhere

The Stairway to Nowhere
References

Burnett, Daniel. "Mythbusters UGA." *The Red and Black*. 28 Jan. 2009. Web. 09 Sept. 2016.

Davis, Melissa. "Ghosts Among the Kudzu." *DigitalCommons@Kennesaw State University*. Kennesaw State University. Web.

French, Jana. "Haunted Places on Campus." *The Red and Black*. 09 Jan. 2015. Web. 09 Sept. 2016.

"Ghost Dawgs." *Ghost Dawgs.Wordpress.com*, Web. 09 Sept. 2016.

Head, Matthew. "Ghosts of Athens, GA (Long but Good!)." *Google Groups*. Newsgroup post. 3 May 1999.

Wehrend, Kyle. "Strange Noises Haunt Campus Halls." *The Red and Black*. 31 Oct. 2001. Web. 09 Sept. 2016.

Wikipedia contributors. "Joseph E. Brown." *Wikipedia, The Free Encyclopedia*. 8 Sep. 2016. Web. 9 Sep. 2016.

Athens Folklore email from the Georgia Ghosts folder in the Hargrett Library collection.

Author interview with a local researcher for the Athens-Clarke Heritage Foundation.

Author interview with Gilbert Head, Archival Associate for the University Archives at the University of Georgia

Author interview with Carol Bishop, Librarian for the University Archives at the University of Georgia

CRESWELL HALL

In 1963, Creswell Hall opened as the University of Georgia's first high-rise residence hall. It is named after Mary Ethel Creswell, the first woman to receive a degree from the University of Georgia.

Located on Baxter Street, the nine-story dormitory is situated close to the heart of the campus. Creswell is a coeducational residential community, in recent years designated solely for first-year students.

One student recalls some unusual events during the years spent living in Creswell hall.

"I moved into Creswell Hall in 1990. It seemed like a typical dorm at first. Later, I noticed electrical anomalies would occur from time to time. I tried to explain them away rationally, but never could.

"The first weird thing that happened was the time I came home to my dorm room in the afternoon after classes. I stood in front of the door and put my key in the lock. As I turned the key, through the door, I heard the answering machine inside. It was playing the outgoing message.

"This was back in the old days when the answering machine was a device with a tape reel that was attached to your land-line phone. When the answering machine picked up, if you were standing there you could hear the outgoing message and when someone left a message, you could hear that, too. So, on the other side of the door, I could hear my voice on the outgoing message saying, "I'm not here right now, please leave a message."

I got the door unlocked and came in. I noticed that I didn't hear anyone leaving a message. The machine had clicked to a stop.

"I pressed the Rewind button so I could hear any messages left on there. Usually, it took only a few seconds to rewind. But, this time, the machine kept on rewinding and rewinding. I looked at it, puzzled, and wondered if it had something wrong with it.

"Finally, it clicked to a stop. I pressed Play. What I heard was my own voice, my outgoing message that said, 'I'm not here right now, please leave a message.' This was weird because normally when someone left a message, the machine didn't ever record or play back that part, the outgoing message. It usually recorded only the voice of the person leaving a message. But this time, as the tape played, it was my voice and my message. And even weirder, it didn't play it back just one time. It played it again and again and again.

"I realized that the reason it had taken so long to rewind was the length of the recording. That it had recorded my outgoing message over and over—about twenty or twenty-five times all together. So, not only was it strange that it would record the outgoing message at all, but that it would record it that many times.

"But, what really made my hair stand on end as I stood there listening to the strange recording play, was when I realized that the recording had stopped itself just as I had put the key into the door. This weird recording had gone on for many minutes as I approached home and then stopped itself just as I came into the room. As if someone unseen had suddenly put a stop to it.

"I remember another incident at Creswell that happened at night. I was startled awake during the night by what sounded like a loud wind in my ears. As I lay in bed trying to pull myself fully from sleep, I listened to the wind noise and wondered what on Earth could be causing it. I was very disoriented. As I tried to make sense of what was happening, I noticed a second sensation. The mattress below me moved as if being depressed, by someone who sat down through my torso and onto the bed.

"At this point I was super freaked out. I lay there for a minute trying to rationalize what was going on, but it just made no sense. I said, 'Screw this!' and jumped up out of the bed.

"I threw on a robe, grabbed my key and a pack of smokes, and left the room. I didn't know what time it was or where I was going, I just had to get out of there. I didn't have a roommate at the time, so it's not like I could commiserate with anyone about it. I rode the elevator down to the lobby, went out back, and smoked a cigarette.

"I was still trying to regain my composure when this giant possum pops out of the bushes right next to me and just looks at me. Those things have always creeped me out, so I was freaked out yet again. I put out my smoke and went back in the building.

"I told myself that I was getting all worked up over nothing and that I needed to just go back up to the room and go to bed. So, I head back to the elevators."

The former student noted that the elevators in Creswell were unusual. It was originally built with six elevators so that every floor of the building starting from the second floor was to have its own lobby. Each lobby was to be serviced, in turn, by one or two elevators, as opposed to all six.

"So, when I lived there, in the lobby there were two elevators next to each other. The one on the right rose only to my floor. The one on the left rose only to the floor above mine. Each elevator went only two places: the lobby and the one designated floor above. This meant that upstairs in the elevator vestibule, one of the elevators never opened. Which one did open depended on which floor you were on. On my floor, the elevator doors on the left never opened. On the floor above, the elevator doors on the right never opened. Everyone just got used to it and always knew which one to use.

"Well, I was waiting for the elevator on the right to go back up to my room. I was still bothered about the weird wind sound that woke me up. I was bothered out about the mattress moving beneath me. I was bothered about the stupid possum. I just wanted to get upstairs, go back to bed, and forget about all of it. The elevator doors opened and I got in.

"Riding up in the elevator, as it approached my floor, I could hear some kids talking as they waited to ride down. The voices approached from above me, then I heard them in front of me, then I heard them below me as the elevator kept going up.

"I was thinking, 'You gotta be kidding me!' So, now, I am in an elevator that has never once gone to the floor above mine. By design. And yet here I was, in that elevator, slowing to a stop on the higher floor. The doors slid open and revealed the number for the floor above mine. I stepped out. I thought, 'Maybe I just got in the wrong elevator because I am tired?' I turned back around and watched as the doors closed on the elevator on the right. 'Nope, that's my regular elevator. It's just on the wrong floor.' I thought.

"I crossed to the stairwell and walked down one flight to my floor. The stairwell door opened onto the elevator vestibule. The kids were still there waiting on the elevator and I heard them complaining about it taking so long to arrive. Apparently, it had gone back to the lobby. I briefly considered telling them what happened to explain why the elevator wasn't there. I decided against it since, if someone told me that happened to them, I'd think they were nuts.

"I made it back to my room, exhausted and confused. I was wary of getting back in that bed, but I was so tired, I did it. Thankfully, I fell asleep and stayed asleep through the night.

The student told me they never saw the elevator do that again and after surreptitious polling of other residents over time, never found anyone else who knew of such a thing happening.

Creswell Hall
References

1101, UGA. ""The '60's: Creswell, Dazed and Confused" by Ethan Hazard." *UGA 1101*: 09 Sept. 2016. Web. 09 Sept. 2016.

"About - University Housing Timeline | University Housing | The University of Georgia." About - University Housing Timeline | University Housing | The University of Georgia. Web. 09 Sept. 2016.

Wikipedia contributors. "Housing at the University of Georgia." *Wikipedia, The Free Encyclopedia*, 15 Jul. 2016. Web. 9 Sep. 2016.

Author interview with a former University of Georgia student

SIGMA NU

The Athens, Georgia chapter of the Sigma Nu fraternity was founded in 1873 as one of the eight original fraternities at the University of Georgia. As the fourth Sigma Nu chapter ever established, it is the oldest continuously-active chapter in the nation.

Sigma Nu succeeded despite anti-fraternity law established by the University of Georgia shortly after its founding, if one can today imagine such a thing. This law stated that any student who joined a Greek letter fraternity would be expelled. However, the law was abandoned in 1881 and the Sigma Nu chapter was re-established.

According to the fraternity's website, Sigma Nu built an impressive French Chateau-style residence at 150 River Road in Athens in 1942. However, several sources for an extraordinary story place a young pledge in the building in 1939. That was the year that William T. Simpson accidentally fell from a second-story window and died.

An article in the *Athens Observer* by Phil Sanderlin details why the Sigma Nu brothers say that Simpson may have crossed over in 1939 to the spirit world, but seems to prefer his old frat house to the Great Beyond.

"Everybody here has heard the story," said Sigma Nu president Rick Ingram. "The legend just sort of floats around here."

Since then, he's made his presence known in various ways, according to the brothers.

"He's supposed to live downstairs in the basement, or what we call 'the Pit,' said Ingram. "There used to be a jukebox down there and it would go on in the middle of the night. Or, a brother would go down to get a Coke from the Coke machine. He'd put in his money and get it. Then, as he's walking up the stairs, he'd hear another bottle drop from the machine. One time, during the Florida weekend, a brother was here by himself and he heard someone playing pool down in the basement. He went downstairs and as he got there, he could even hear the clack of the cue. When he walked in, nobody was there. But, he said the pool balls were in motion. Also, sometimes the lights in the basement go on. We figure any ghost who likes music, drinks Cokes, and plays pool can't be all bad."

The ghost pledge still takes an active interest in fraternity affairs. Ingram commented, "When a new president is elected, it's said that if the ghost likes him, he'll put the guy's shoes against the wall during the night. If he doesn't like the new president, he'll turn his shoes over."

The plaque which commemorates Simpson's death has a way of disappearing and reappearing, too. Ingram said: "His plaque still pops up now and then. I just came across it once. Just opened a door and there it was."

Skeptics will point out that all of the manifestations mentioned in this article are quite capable of being produced by imagination or some human agent. Of course, it's easy not to believe in ghosts. That is, it's easy in the broad daylight.

"Sometimes," said Ingram, "we hear noises at night down in the Pit. Nobody says they really believe in ghosts. Still, nobody wants to go see what it is."

Gayle Peeples' article "Ghost Story" in the *Georgia Impression* offers more details:

> The brothers guess that the boy had been performing typical pledge duties for the fraternity Commander, because it was from the Commander's window that he fell. Since then, brothers have sworn that the ghost has appeared to them, usually in the 'Pit', or basement. When one of the brothers would approach the young man's apparition, it would quickly vanish.
>
> The house on River Road made Sigma Nu member Dennis Crews a true believer in the ghost's existence. Crews pointed out that his own skepticism dissolved after experiencing the portent's mischief first hand. During fall quarter of 1970, Crews and another Sigma Nu were alone in the house studying for finals. 'I had been up studying until midnight,' he related. 'At about 5 a.m. I just woke up—I don't know why—and I heard this tapping, like a steady rhythm, at my window.' He said the tapping would stop, then start again. Thinking it was only the wind, Crews peered out his window into the darkness; there were no ledges or tree limbs outside to allow access to his room. The tapping persisted, so Crews went in search of his fraternity brother. Finding him studying in the next room, Crews exclaimed, 'So you're the one making those noises!' Suddenly the two brothers heard noises overhead, as if someone were walking in the attic. 'I ran upstairs, flipped on the light, and—no one was there,' Crews attested. At this point, he noted that the fraternity keeps old composites of past memberships hanging on the attic walls. Now, however, Crews noticed that many of these were scattered about the floor.
>
> Downstairs again, the brothers began discussing the mysterious happenings when they heard the back door open and close on the main floor below them. Footsteps could then be heard proceeding up three steps toward the second floor. Relieved that another brother had returned, they ran downstairs and encountered

only an empty foyer. Crews quickly checked the door and found it unlocked. 'I remembered locking that door,' he said, 'but we searched the entire house and no one else was there.'

The real clincher, Crews feels, happens whenever the ghost is seen or heard, because the plaque which commemorates his death curiously disappears, sometimes for as long as two or three weeks. 'It was gone that night when we looked for it,' Crews stated, 'and it turned up two weeks later.'

The brothers have been told that the spirit is a friendly one and he roams the house, frustrated because he was never initiated into the fraternity.

One quirk about the Sigma Nu residence was that, although the fraternity owned the building, the River Road land it rested on was owned by the University of Georgia, who leased the property to them. In the year 2000, an electrical fire started in an upstairs bedroom of the house. No one was hurt, but the fraternity members had to relocate. After the University implemented new structural and electrical regulations, the house, which was one of the largest and oldest on campus, could not be restored to meet the new safety requirements.

Although they lost the historic home, they broke ground on a new chapter house on River Road during Fall 2008 and completed construction in 2009. Construction was finished August 1, 2009 and the chapter now resides in the New Chateau on River Road.

"We couldn't be more pleased to return to River Road, where we were for more than 50 years," said Michael Barry, a member of Sigma Nu's Home Association.

One wonders if William Simpson made the move to the new home as well. If so, I feel sure the members still make him feel right at home.

Sigma Nu
References

Peeples, Gayle. "Ghost Story." Georgia Impression. Vol 7 Number 1. (Undated clipping from the Georgia Ghosts folder in the Hargrett Library collection.)

Head, Matthew. "Ghosts of Athens, GA (Long but Good!)." *Google Groups*. Newsgroup post. 3 May 1999.

Sanderlin, Phil. "The haunting: Several Athens houses have legends of ghosts and noises in the night." The *Athens Observer*. October 30, 1980. (Clipping from the Georgia Ghosts folder in the Hargrett Library collection.)

Shearer, Lee. "UGA's Money Goes for Off-campus Digs." *http://onlineathens.com/*. *Athens Banner-Herald*, Web.

"Sigma Nu." UGA Interfraternity Council. *The Interfraternity Council of the University of Georgia*. Web. 09 Sept. 2016.

"Sigma Nu History - UGA." *UGASigmaNu.com*. Web. 09 Sept. 2016.

PHI MU

Phi Mu has the distinction of being the first sorority at the University of Georgia. With the admission of women to the University in 1920, Mary Lyndon became the first dean of women and also founded the Alpha Alpha Chapter of Phi Mu, the 27th chapter to be chartered in the nation.

The Phi Mu sorority house at 250 South Milledge Avenue is also known as the Hamilton-Phinizy-Segrest House. In 1857, the Greek Revival home was built for Colonel Thomas Napier Hamilton, reputed to be Georgia's first millionaire. Previous residents of the fashionable downtown Athens Lickskillet neighborhood, the Hamiltons were among the first to build a home on Milledge Avenue. The house featured the first bathtub in Athens.

Tracy Coley Ingram's article in the *Athens Banner-Herald*, "Classic Places: Home of Georgia's first millionaire," describes the home's history:

> The son of James Hamilton, a captain of the American Revolution, Hamilton graduated from the University of Georgia in 1807 and was a University trustee from 1834 to 1851. When he passed away in 1858 at age 70, his son, James Hamilton, oversaw

construction using slave labor and featuring an intricately detailed ironwork, supposedly shipped from Philadelphia on the last train to come through before secession. James' mother, Sarah, lived in the home until her death in 1876.

Afterward, the home was then rented to Dr. and Mrs. H. C. White, who were possibly the most preeminent couple on the Athens social scene at that time. The Whites frequently had house guests from the North, who were said to have shocked Athens citizens "from center to circumference" with their behavior. One female visitor from Baltimore was invited by a local gentleman to go horseback riding, and when he arrived he found her riding astride on a man's saddle! The Whites later had yet another female house guest from Baltimore, and she nearly caused a riot when she rode through town on a bicycle in her bloomers.

In 1890, James Hamilton passed away, and the home was sold to the widow of Ferdinand Phinizy, who spent a considerable amount of money on a Victorian remodel. She installed gas chandeliers, stained-glass windows, marble mantel tops, golden oak paneling and silk damask wall coverings.

Mrs. Robert Segrest, granddaughter of Mrs. Phinizy, obtained the home upon Mrs. Phinizy's death. She lived in the home until 1964 when she sold it to the Phi Mu sorority.

The sorority undertook renovations, including adding new wings, a dormitory, and replacing entry stairs. Athens historic preservation expert Albert Sams oversaw the main stairwell replacement and gifted the sorority two new hand-carved replica mantels for the parlors. In an elaborate final touch, housemother Madge Haney obtained in New Orleans a four-and-a-half-foot tall, five-foot diameter crystal chandelier with 48 lights.

Despite the ritzy new Victorian trappings, the sorority house cannot escape its own past.

According to folklore, previous owner Charles Phinizy had an affair with a woman named Anna Powell (or Anna Hamilton, by some accounts). Anna was married as well, and worried that Phinizy was about to expose their affair to her husband. To silence him, Anna attempted to shoot Phinizy but fainted in the process. Upon regaining consciousness, she found that her bullet had not found its intended target but rather killed her unfortunate husband, James Harris.

Rumor has it the hapless husband was buried under the stairs of the home. The fact that no gravestone nor record of his death has been found encourages this belief.

In the summer of 1969, Phi Mu sorority member Barbara Poulos and her friends attempted to trace these families and document the pieces of the story. Gayle Peeples' article "Ghost Story" in the *Georgia Impression* offers more details:

> Both the Hamilton and Phinizy family trees were located in the Annals of Athens, where Anna's marriage to Harris was also chronicled. The gravesites of each family were discovered in local cemeteries, but curiously missing was the tomb of Harris. At this point Barbara interjected that when the house was remodeled the plot under these steps was left undisturbed. If Harris's grave were buried there it was never unearthed.
>
> The girls found the descendants of Anna and Phinizy extremely reluctant to discuss the truth behind the legend. And no record of the murder exists in the old Athens newspapers—in fact, Barbara found that the microfilm copies of Harris's death and of the following day were strangely missing.
>
> Since their initial discovery of the aristocratic spook, occupants of the old house have witnessed her ghostly antics and indeed, may have stumbled upon a possible accomplice to Anna. During that summer a coed reported awakening, for no apparent reason, in the middle of the night. There, standing before her closed

bedroom door, was the figure of a young man dressed in full Confederate uniform. As she stared unbelievingly, the apparition faded and vanished.

None of the girls claim to have seen Anna's ghost, but several have reported sounds of a woman crying in the vicinity of the front staircase. When one of the braver sisters went to investigate, the crying suddenly ceased and she encountered only a deserted foyer. The girls vow however, that late at night, when no lights shine inside the house, the distinct form of a cross can be seen on the floor of the entrance, presumably marking the spot where Harris was killed.

Barbara's faith in Anna's presence might not be so staunch had she not witnessed ghostly communication herself. Barbara related that she went downstairs to a small kitchenette located in the old section of the house. At this time, only Barbara and two other sisters were staying there as final exam week was ending. Suddenly, Barbara heard three deliberate raps, as if someone was knocking on the wall behind her. Running upstairs to ask the other girls if they had made the sound, she found them both asleep.

Barbara remains convinced that those raps can only be explained by the presence of an unearthly being.

In addition, late one night, a girl witnessed a door unlocked for her by unseen hands.

A Phi Mu member experienced a fright, as told to Nancy Roberts in her book *Georgia Ghosts*: "One time, I heard someone sobbing their heart out. It sounded so close when I stood near the stairs, and I looked everywhere thinking it was a sorority member I might be able to comfort. But there was absolutely no one there—no one on the whole floor."

When previous Phi Mu president Janet French was asked if she believes in ghosts, she replied, "I reckon I do. I've seen the cross at the bottom of the stairs." She said the sisters don't really regard the house specter as menacing. "When we start talking about it, we get goosebumps," she said. "But, we aren't scared of it." (Sanderlin)

The Hamilton-Phinizy-Segrest House was designated a historic landmark on Jan. 8, 1991. As long as it stands, the truth about what happened between Anna and James inside the house may never be known.

Phi Mu
References

Coley, Tracy. "Classic Places: Home of Georgia's First Millionaire." *Onlineathens.com. Athens Banner-Herald.* Web.

Davis, Melissa. "Ghosts Among the Kudzu." *DigitalCommons@Kennesaw State University.* Kennesaw State University. Web.

Head, Matthew. "Ghosts of Athens, GA (Long but Good!)." *Google Groups.* Newsgroup post. 3 May 1999.

Peeples, Gayle. "Ghost Story." *Georgia Impression.* Vol 7 Number 1. (Undated clipping from the Georgia Ghosts folder in the Hargrett Library collection.)

Roberts, Nancy. *Georgia Ghosts.* Winston-Salem N.C.: John F. Blair, 1997. Print.

Sanderlin, Phil. "The haunting: Several Athens houses have legends of ghosts and noises in the night." *The Athens Observer.* October 30, 1980. (Clipping from the Georgia Ghosts folder in the Hargrett Library collection.)

The Athens-Clarke Heritage Foundation Walking Tour. http://www.athenswelcomecenter.com/images/milledge_ave_walking_tour.pdf

SIGMA PHI EPSILON

Sigma Phi Epsilon, located at 327 South Milledge Avenue, is reported to have a spectral member. Fraternity member Daniel Fields, recalls this tale in Elizabeth Howard's *Red and Black* article:

> "Supposedly, rumor has it that, a long time ago the owner of the house was crazy and had a bad day. He came back after work and drowned his daughter in the bathtub and then killed himself. They never found his body, though. The daughter, Tabitha, supposedly haunts the house.
>
> "There have been multiple stories, but the most recent one goes like this: Timothy S. was sitting in one of the rooms and heard some noise in the loft. He figured it was one of his roommates just messing around, so he shrugged it off. He then heard something that sounded like a little girl crying. To make sure everyone was okay, he yelled up the loft. No one responded. He then went up to the loft to find out that no one was in the loft. The TV was on with only one channel playing static."

Members described their experiences to Ashlee Davis in *The Red and Black*:

"I lived in room No. 2 my entire sophomore year and there were many, many kinds of weird things that would happen throughout the year, whether it was flickering lights or seeing things that weren't where we left them," said Jeff Ostenson, a recent marketing graduate from Stone Mountain.

Sigma Phi Epsilon's haunted story begins with a family who lived in the house prior to the fraternity. The father — who was in some variations a priest and in others a chemistry professor from the University named H.G. White — was fired from his job.

In a fit of madness, he drowned his young daughter, Tabitha, in the upstairs bathroom. According to rumor, he either hung himself in the attic or disappeared altogether, never to be seen again.

"Ever since then the house has been haunted by Tabitha," said Jim Martin, a fifth-year psychology major from Alpharetta.

Several fraternity brothers have come forward with unexplained occurrences — a ball bouncing, footsteps in the attic and the echo of a girl's laughter — all of which were supposedly done at the mischievous hands of Tabitha.

Ostenson recalls a particularly unnerving event after closing his bedroom door.

"It wasn't five minutes after we had done that the door slowly creaked open," Ostenson said. "Obviously you can't make a door creaking noise in the paper, but it was the worst door creak noise ever."

He and his roommate, Wes Robertson, quickly looked down at the door to find no one standing at the threshold. Then it slammed shut.

"It slammed while we were watching the door and I never had anything like that happen," Ostenson said.

Neither roommate could offer an explanation for the door opening and promptly closing.

"It's one of those doors that doesn't catch," said Robertson, a finance graduate from Memphis, Tenn.

The stories don't end there. Robertson and Ostenson both recall lights turning off by themselves, which Ostenson claims was not a result of a simple power surge.

"Out of nowhere all the lights got very noticeably brighter, like all of them were about double the brightness, and then they all burned out," Ostenson said. "I knew it wasn't a power surge or anything because the TV was still on, the TV was still working. But I went around and tried all the lights, and all of my bulbs had to be replaced."

In addition to the standard spooks of flickering lights and self-shutting doors, residents returned to their room to find personal items in odd places.

"No moving beds or anything, but I would set down my phone and literally just walk to my dresser and come back and it wouldn't be where I thought I set it down," Ostenson said.

Other experiences were on the more subtle side of eerie.

"I'd come back to sit down and study, and get on my laptop and something just didn't feel like it was in the right place," Martin said. "I couldn't really put my finger on it. It never really stuck out like my printer's on the other side of the room or something, but it wouldn't be the way it was when I left it."

Residents note being spooked on a psychological level as well, reporting feelings of unease when alone in the house and plagues of strange dreams.

"I just had some really weird dreams while I was sleeping there, a lot more than I had at other times or other places," Robertson said.

Just how much of this ghost story can be chalked up to the unknown? First a little must be known about the house's history.

Property records at the Athens-Clarke County courthouse indicate that the house changed hands twice since being built in 1950. Its most recent sale was in 1975 when Alpha Xi Delta sold the property to Sigma Phi Epsilon.

According to the deed book, the earliest warranty deed was in 1959, when Alpha Xi Delta bought the property from Omchap, a housing corporation.

But as to who lived in the house before either fraternity? Not even a ghost of a record remains.

Though the history of the house prior to 1959 is murky, explanation for the origin of this story is not so otherworldly.

Reasonable explanation or not, many fraternity members insist that it's possible there is something amiss.

"I'm not big on ghosts or anything, but you never know," Robertson said. "They were kind of freaky when you think about them in retrospect."

Sigma Phi Epsilon References

Howard, Elizabeth. "The Haunted (Greek) Houses of UGA." *The Red and Black.* 05 Sept. 2013. Web. 09 Sept. 2016.

WADDEL HALL

Waddel Hall near Jackson Street on North Campus is older than any other University of Georgia building except Old College. Completed in 1821, the federal-style building was originally known as Philosophical Hall because it stored books and equipment for the sciences, called "natural philosophy" at that time. The building was later renamed for educator and University president Moses Waddel.

Moses Waddel was born in North Carolina in 1770 and by age 14, he was a teacher at local schools. While in college in Virginia, he fell in love with Eliza Pleasants. However, Eliza's father disapproved of their plans to live in Georgia and the relationship ended.

While teaching in Abbeville, South Carolina, Waddel married Catherine Calhoun. However, they were married only one year before Catherine and their infant daughter both died. In 1800, Waddel reunited with Eliza Pleasants. Upon finding out that Eliza had never married, he proposed and they were married.

By 1819, Waddel accepted the post as the fifth President of the University of Georgia, which by Waddel's account, had seven students and three professors at that time. Waddel increased enrollment to one hundred students, secured funds to build a library and three other buildings: Philosophical Hall in 1821, New College in 1823, and Demosthenian Hall in 1824. Waddel resigned in 1829 and passed away in 1840.

Philosophical Hall was utilized for the new Agriculture and Mechanics College classrooms until 1874. After the A&M college departed, University treasurer and registrar Thomas W. Reed lived in the building in the early 1900s. In 1918, the hall was known as the Road Laboratory Building. The upper floor was student housing, while the lower floor stored supplies for science classes such as telescopes, barometers and other instruments. At one point, the building was used as a gymnasium.

The A&M college returned to the building in the early '40s and it was renamed Agricultural Hall. Here, cream from the University's cows was stored, which led to students sneaking in at night to drink the cream. As Tracy Ingram's *Athens Banner-Herald* article states, "More than one young man was found with his head stuck in the milk can waiting to be rescued from the cream he had so coveted." At that point, the building was completely open with no partitions and students from the dairy school made butter there. To this day, the building retains the original circular ventilator from this period.

The building was remodeled in 1955 and renamed Waddel Hall in honor of Moses Waddel. Over the next decades, the hall was used by the speech therapy department, the Dean Rusk Center, the University president, and the Vice President for Government Relations. Today, Waddel Hall houses the Office of Special Events.

In 1918, when the upper story rooms were rented out to students, an event occurred that forever changed the way people thought of Waddel Hall. Students and community members alike were horrified.

Twenty-year-old Jamie Johnson of Jefferson, Georgia, had recently returned from France, where he served in World War I. He had come to Athens on the evening of Tuesday, January 29, 1918, to speak with 17-year-old Belle Hill, who had been his girlfriend. Between 11 p.m. and midnight on the cold rainy night, the pair were seen conversing in the Manhaton Café at 114 College Avenue. Neither of the young people were enrolled at the University of Georgia.

They met there, ostensibly, to discuss the breakup of their relationship after Belle had fallen for another man while Jamie was away at war. Between 2 a.m. and 3 a.m., the discussion moved to Waddel Hall where a mutual acquaintance was boarding. They all crashed in a room leased by Alva Pendergrass, Howard Dadisman, and Tom Holliday.

The tenants were jolted awake when three gunshots rang out. When they discovered that Jamie had shot Belle and then killed himself, they went to the New York Cafe on Clayton Street to use the phone to call the police. The murder-suicide was the first recorded murder on campus.

The Athens Banner published Jaime Johnson's despondent suicide note which asked for forgiveness and listed his outstanding debts. "...my burden is so great I can't go with it any further," he declared. Very little has ever been published about the incident, but the 1918 UGA Faculty Minutes record that both bodies were found lying on the floor, completely nude.

Rumors ran amok in Athens when the three tenants left town, but in truth, they were in Jefferson visiting Johnson's widowed mother, whom all three knew. They reported to her in person the details of what occurred that night. Rumors further supposed that Belle had been pregnant with Jamie's illegitimate child, but this was not substantiated.

Historians would have loved to hear that account! Much debate remains about whether or not the three tenants were actually inside the rental when the shots were fired. First, a coroner's inquest verified how the two young people died. Then, a Clarke County Grand Jury cleared Pendergrass, Holliday, and Dadisman of any criminal wrongdoing, although, all three were dismissed from the University for "knowingly permitting an unmarried couple to enter their room and disrobe for the night and occupy said room with said students."

"Then, it was such a disgrace to be caught in bed with a girl overnight, and today, I guess it'd be a disgrace not to be," quipped University historian Nash Boney.

Belle and Jamie are both buried in their respective family plots in Jackson County.

Since these tragic events, some who spend time in Waddel Hall report unusual activity. People working in offices located there claim unnatural chills or fleeting glimpses of "something." Others report hearing strange noises at night or sounds of the tragic lovers' quarrel being replayed over and over.

Waddel Hall

Waddel Hall
References

Athens-Clarke Heritage Room. "30 January 1918: Murder-Suicide on UGA Campus." *This Day in Athens:* Web. 09 Sept. 2016.

Bishop, Carol. "Haunted North Campus Walking Tour Script". Athens-Clarke Heritage Foundation tour on July 20, 2010.

Conway, Lindsey. "Over the Dog Years: North Campus Buildings a Time Capsule of UGA History." *The Red and Black*. 30 Apr. 2015. Web. 09 Sept. 2016.

Davis, Melissa. "Ghosts Among the Kudzu." *DigitalCommons@Kennesaw State University*. Kennesaw State University. Web.

Gottlieb, Jamie. "University Historian Uncovers Hidden Tales of Georgia." *The Red and Black*, 05 Mar. 2013. Web. 09 Sept. 2016.

Head, Matthew. "Ghosts of Athens, GA (Long but Good!)." *Google Groups*. Newsgroup post. 3 May 1999.

Ingram, Tracy Coley. "Classic Places: Waddel Hall Has Served Many Purposes." *Online Athens. Athens Banner-Herald*, n.d. Web. 09 Sept. 2016.

"Waddel Hall." Buildings & Locations. Web. 09 Sept. 2016. <http://www.uga.edu/a-z/location/waddel-hall/>.

"Waddel Hall - Wikimapia." Waddel Hall. *Wikimapia.org*, 2011. Web. 09 Sept. 2016.

Wikipedia contributors. "Moses Waddel." *Wikipedia, The Free Encyclopedia*. 17 Jul. 2016. Web. 9 Sep. 2016.

Wilkes, Donald E. Jr., "Tragic Tale Recounts First Murder on UGA Campus" (1992). Popular Media. Paper 142. *http://digitalcommons.law.uga.edu/fac_pm/142*

Athens Folklore email from the Georgia Ghosts folder in the Hargrett Library collection.

Author interview with Gilbert Head, Archival Associate for the University Archives at the University of Georgia

HISTORIC ATHENS

THE MORTON THEATRE

The Morton Theatre, located at 195 West Washington Street in downtown Athens is listed in the National Register of Historic Places as one of the oldest surviving vaudeville theaters in the United States which was built, owned, and operated by an African-American.

African-American businessman Monroe Bowers "Pink" Morton was born in Athens in May of 1853. As a successful contractor, Pink built the Wilkes County Courthouse in Washington, Georgia. Active in his community, Pink Morton was chosen as a delegate to the Republican National Convention in 1896 and in 1897, was appointed as the U.S. Postmaster of Athens, Georgia.

Pink began construction on the Morton Building in 1909 and opened for business on May 18, 1910. Morton had designed the structure himself using reclaimed architectural elements. No two columns holding up the second-story seating area in the theater were alike.

The Morton Building was home to not only the 500-seat Morton Theatre, but also businesses, including the first African-American-owned drugstore in Athens (E.D. Harris Drug Store) and the dental practice of the first licensed African-American female dentist (Dr. Ida Johnson Hiram).

The Morton Theatre's opening act was Alice Carter Simmons, an African-American pianist who studied at the Oberlin Conservatory. Famous acts that played the Morton include Cab Calloway, Bessie Smith, Louis Armstrong, and Duke Ellington.

The Morton was one of the main anchors of Hot Corner, a commercial district of downtown Athens at the intersection of Washington and Hull Streets that was the center of African-American life in Athens. It was known as Hot Corner because there was no modern heating and air conditioning. As artists performed inside the Morton, "...the windows were up and music inside spilled out into the streets," according to Lynn Green, Facilities Supervisor at the Morton Theater. "The Hot Corner was the hip, happening place to be."

Despite being one of Athens' wealthiest citizens, Pink Morton was hands-on with shows in the theater, often running lighting or acting as the stage director. Pink recorded his position as a "switchboard operator" in now-faded paint on a backstage wall. In graffiti on the backstage dressing room walls, someone scrawled a graphic statement about smoking regulations and the consequences of breaking them. (This piece of wall is currently displayed in the museum area in upper lobby of the theater.)

By 1914, Morton was the owner, publisher, and editor of the Progressive Era, a local black newspaper. Sadly, Pink Morton died five years later at the age of 66. At the time of his death, Morton owned nearly thirty buildings throughout the city.

Over the following years, many tenants called the Morton Building home, including insurance companies, pool halls, restaurants, a bakery, and even a few mortuaries.

When vaudeville fell out of style, it operated as a burlesque house. In the 1930s, the theater was modified to be a movie house. A projection booth was added on the second floor to replace the original upper-level gallery.

When the Fire Marshal investigated, he discovered that the 700-seat theater had only one door in and one door out, and closed down the theater for failing to offer adequate emergency exits. While the theater remained closed for the next 40 years, other businesses on the ground floor of the Morton Building continued operations.

The building remained in the Morton family until 1973, when it was sold. Although the theater and most of the upper-level offices were neglected, the Morton Building continued to house a beauty salon, a bookstore, a restaurant, and a photo lab. At this time during the 1970s, the building housed the El Dorado cafe, a vegetarian restaurant that employed members of the band The B-52's before they were famous.

In 1980, the Morton Building was purchased by the nonprofit Morton Theatre Corporation. At that time, local bands The B-52's and R.E.M. occasionally used the building to rehearse. Later, R.E.M. filmed part of their music video for "The One I Love" in the Morton Theatre.

In 1987, Athens-Clarke County funding allowed the restoration of the theater, including repairs to the collapsed roof.

In 1991, the Athens-Clarke County gained ownership of the Morton Building and in the fall of 1993, after a 1.8-million-dollar renovation, the Morton Theatre was reopened. Seating 490 patrons, the Morton again became a community performing arts center hosting live theater, music concerts, weddings, seminars, pageants, awards shows, and other community events.

Since its restoration, some employees and visitors have had experiences they have trouble explaining.

"Old theaters are a little on the creepy side," opined local historian Jeff Clarke. Regarding the fire of 1932 in the Morton, he suggests, "It's suspected that an employee of the theater left a lit cigar on some boxes backstage. Today, although employees strictly enforce the No Smoking policy, the strong scent of cigar smoke can be smelled in the building from time to time."

A former employee of the Morton Theatre spent a great deal of time in the building, starting in the Spring of 2010. "I was there alone a lot. It's really creepy," she told me.

"There had been several instances where ghost hunters had gone to the Morton and they always say it's filled with stuff. But, I'm a little skeptical about that, too," she confided.

"Things at the Morton supposedly happened all the time. People would say 'I saw somebody walking up the stairs and then he disappeared.' I was always skeptical, unless it happened to me."

She recalled one story in particular from her days at the Morton. "An outside worker brought his child to work with him, doing some freelance finishing. His daughter was playing around downstairs [as he worked on the catwalk above the stage]. He looked down and his daughter was sitting with another child on the stage, seemingly playing. He wondered, 'What is this kid doing there?' When he went down to check it out and see who the kid was, there was no other child."

This was not the only time a spectral child visited the Morton. "There were a lot of children seen in there. You don't know if that had something to do with the crematorium that had been down there. There were funerals in the funeral parlors there."

"People using the back stage have claimed to see children. A child was often seen running to the light booth. But, it wasn't always a light booth.

It had been storage space for props. It is surmised that long ago they used children as costume runners to go get things."

She also recalled hearing about an event that took place just before she began working at the Morton. A photo shoot had been arranged to take pictures for the 100-year anniversary of the Morton Theatre. A photographer was trying to take photos of someone on stage who was posing as if they were giving a performance.

"The cameras were all set up, but the photographer could not get any of the cameras to go off to take the picture. There was some kind of technical difficulty." After trying unsuccessfully several times, they stood examining the equipment wondering what the issue could be. "Then, Pow! Pow! Pow! All the cameras went off at once and took the photos."

The photographer claimed that there was another figure that was an apparition in the digital photos taken. "I tried to track the photos down, but could not," she said.

This Morton employee not only heard stories about strange events, she witnessed some as well.

"It's an old building and there can be a tendency for leaks. A leak over the stage can be devastating to equipment. So, you always do a walk through in the morning just to see if anything happened. There's a series of lights you always turn on as you walk through the different areas because it's really dark. But, the energy that is burned when all the theater lights are on is really expensive, so you're always turning lights off when you leave a room. I would turn on the light and start walking, but then the light would go off. You certainly notice it when they go off and you are in the middle of the stage. I thought, 'Really!? Seriously!?'

"[At the end of the day] when you're walking out of the theater, you turn the lights off and it goes dark. You walk out and boom! The lights come back up. It wasn't something like you would walk out and had just forgotten to turn off the lights. They come on gradually and you would watch them come back on.

Lights in the theater coming on and going off by themselves happened on occasion, she said. "Not every day. Enough so it was like, 'Again??!!' I guess one could say, 'It's an old building.' But, it had a pretty sophisticated lighting system. A lot of emotion would have happened in that theater. For whatever reason, it's probably some kind of hot spot."

Jeff Montgomery has worked in the Athens-Clarke County Public Information office for 18 years, acting as the Public Information Officer for the last two years. His responsibilities include running the government access television channel and creating videos with information about Athens-Clarke County. When I spoke with Mr. Montgomery, he described a short film his office produced about the Morton. Drawing on his interest in the paranormal, Jeff decided to film an investigation there.

"I had heard stories about the Morton. With Fall approaching, I thought we could conduct an overnight ghost hunt and do a piece for the local channel about the Morton Theatre ghosts that would be fun and interesting for viewers," he explained. It was also a chance to inform the citizens of Athens about the building's history.

Prior to the investigation, the Morton Theatre provided some contact information for people who had had experiences in the theater. They arranged to interview them about their experiences, and portions of their interviews are described below:

Ricky Whitlock

Ricky Whitlock has been an employed by Athens-Clarke County since 1993. "When Athens-Clarke County took over the building, a couple of stories came with the building that we were told.

"An electrician came in on a Saturday with his four-year-old daughter. They were up on the stage where he was doing some wiring. He saw the girl waving.

"When he noticed this, he asked 'Who are you waving at?' She answered, 'The man on the beam.' She pointed up at the light fixtures up in the ceiling.

"The electrician looked up, then told her, 'There's nobody there.' The girl said, 'Yes, daddy, there's an elderly man with a beard and overalls.'"

"The second story we were told about was that there was a welder working in the same area that the little girl had seen the gentleman in the ceiling.

"As he worked, he stopped to check his weld. He raised his shield up, and suddenly got the sense that somebody was looking at him and he looked up. Well, the welder left the building.

"Later, he told his friends he worked with that there was an elderly black man with a beard and overalls sitting right next to his weld, watching him. He swore he would not come back in the Morton building ever again."

(Ricky points up toward the ceiling) "This opening right here where the lights are, is where both events occurred.

"The guy said his daughter told him the man's feet were hanging down in the air through the opening where the lights shine down on the stage cause he was working on a set of lights that were actually on the stage. The daughter was waving up into that hole. So, he was on that catwalk. That's where the welder was. He was welding the catwalk when he saw him."

"If I was looking for ghosts in this building, I would start on the catwalk in the attic."

A Former Employee

A former employee of Athens-Clarke County worked in the Morton Theatre. She conducted an early morning walk through at the theater. "I turned off the light and went to walk out, and the light turned back on as I was standing there, which was a little disconcerting," she confided.

"I turned around and I looked, and I turned it off again. I turned to leave and it turned back on, which was really, really odd. I thought 'I hope we don't have some kind of electrical issue.'

"I looked out towards the stage and I see a blue light emanating from stage left. It was a pulsating, blue, very bright light. Now, this auditorium was very dark. And, even though we have blackout shades, sometimes you can see headlights coming through there. This was not like that.

"This was on the stage and it almost had a sound. It was really bizarre. So, I thought, okay, having not learned anything from old horror movies, I went to investigate.

"I took my flashlight and went up on to the stage. The light was in the corner and then it disappeared. I went and turned on the stage lights and I was trying to find any place where there could have been lights leaking through. There was nothing."

"The other story that is very interesting is that somebody is seen looking out of the light booth. And that's sort of strange because that light booth was not always there. In the early part of the twentieth century, the Morton was a movie house. The prop room was where the projection room would have been.

"Somebody who worked for the Fox Institute in Atlanta visited because they were helping fund the restoration project. The representative was checking on the status of the project.

"She was up in the balcony and she could feel somebody watching her. She looked in the window and there was a man standing there, staring at her. But, there was nobody there. The person kind of just faded away. She was totally, totally freaked out.

"But, it goes along with what other people have seen time and time again. That there is somebody walking around, peering out from that booth. It is an apparition that has been seen several times over the years."

Joyce Reifsteck

Joyce Reifsteck was employed by the Morton Theatre as an Events Coordinator. "During my time at the Morton, I did have some very unusual experiences," Joyce declared.

"Probably the most profound one happened one day when I was planning a Morton event and had to go meet a caterer at their warehouse. I left my two-and-a-half-year-old son at home with his babysitter.

"While I was gone, the babysitter put my son down for a nap. She then needed to run out to her car to get a book. The girl dashed out to the car and didn't even have shoes on. She just grabbed her car keys, ran out, got the book, and upon returning, she realized that she had locked herself out of the house.

"What's interesting is I never take a phone call during a meeting. But, for some reason, when I felt that buzzing in my pocket, I thought, 'I better take this call.'

"This frantic babysitter is on the line explaining how she left my baby at my house alone and that she is downtown looking for me.

"All of a sudden, I became absolutely calm. And, I said, 'It's okay. Settle down. Drive back to the house and my husband will meet you there.'

"Within ten minutes, everybody was at the house. My husband checked on the baby and everything was fine. The babysitter was panicky and teary and thought she'd lost her job. But, it all ended up okay.

"Later that evening when I was putting my son to bed, he said, 'Mommy...Kelly left me today.'

"I said, 'Well, she didn't leave you...she accidentally locked herself out of the house.' He said, 'Mommy, it was okay, because Pink came and he watched me the whole time that Kelly was gone until Daddy got home.'

"I don't know if you can see this on camera (she points to goosebumps on her arm) but, just telling that story, I almost cry every time. It chills me because my son was two-and-a-half! He had no knowledge of where I worked or who Pink Morton was.

"He has talked about that several times since, about how that man named Pink came and stayed with him when the babysitter went away."

Joyce continued, "In one of the back dressing rooms, you get the sensation of a little child running around. People have heard him laughing, people have heard him talking. He'll run away and hide from you. I've always personally gotten the sensation of a little mop-haired boy. A lot of people have said the same thing, that they have felt the presence of a child back there.

"There's a place through here on this aisle where there is a cold spot. And, the more you talk about it, the colder it gets. Many people have experienced that cold spot, when the air conditioner is on, when the air conditioner is not on. A lot of people say that they feel some sort of presence right over here (she gestures to the aisle.)"

Mr. Montgomery had a contact on the Georgia Haunt Hunt team who, in turn, contacted the Ghosts of Georgia paranormal investigators.

"The Ghosts of Georgia paranormal investigators had previously investigated the Eagle Tavern in Watkinsville and a friend of mine vouched that they conducted themselves professionally," he said.

Mr. Montgomery teamed up with six investigators with Ghosts of Georgia and a Radar Productions videographer to conduct an overnight investigation. They set up a variety of recording equipment and walked through the 104-year-old building. "There were no tax dollars at work for this project," Montgomery specified. "The investigation was free."

Jeff Montgomery and the team of investigators set up a monitoring room in the administrative offices at the front of the theater. Investigators recorded base readings for temperature and electrical magnetic field (EMF).

Additional investigative tools used included voice recorders, light grids, video cameras, and a thermal camera. Cameras were placed to watch the stage, the theater seats, the catwalk lights, the balcony, and the production booth.

Mr. Montgomery points out that the investigation did take place in downtown Athens on a Saturday night. Although a home football game was not scheduled in town that night, there was usual weekend activity going on outside the theater, such as people and cars passing by. This meant that many things could be explained away: a light was a passing car, a noise that was a person close by outside talking loudly.

Other evidence from the investigation was not so easily dismissed.

Mr. Montgomery personally witnessed orbs of light that were visible in the theater but could not be explained. To him, the most interesting evidence was the audio obtained. The investigative team captured audio evidence when no one was in the building or when no one was in the area where it was captured.

In one case, cameras and audio equipment were set up all around the theater. Then, everyone left the building for a while except those who remained inside the monitoring room.

When everyone returned they reviewed the recordings made while they had been gone. The devices had recorded the sound of a person whistling inside the theater. This has occurred during the time when no one was inside the theater and the people in the monitoring room were nowhere near the theater.

"That's interesting and hard to explain," Mr. Montgomery noted.

Another piece of audio captured inside the theater was a recording of the voice of a woman yelling and telling people to get out.

Some investigators saw shadows and heard voices for which they weren't sure about the origins.

I asked Mr. Montgomery if the experience was frightening or benign.

"No one felt threatened or like we shouldn't be here," He replied. "But when you are down in the former bloodletting room of a mortuary, it's a little weird."

"It's creepy in the sense that you are in the very back room of the dressing room area in a dark basement. There are narrow brick walkways down there that haven't changed a lot over the years. It's eerie."

Actors performing at the Morton have reported odd activity in the dressing room.

"At one point, there were three of us in the basement. It's completely black and there is no light coming in anywhere. We were sitting in that blackness asking questions. While we asked the questions, we heard a large thump on the stage above us. We knew no one was supposed to be on the stage at that time. When we checked it out, no one was up there. We couldn't figure out what that was.

"There is no confirmation that anyone died in the theater or met a tragic end in the building at any point in its history. It was a place of entertainment where people came to have a good time and be entertained. It was a popular venue and has positive vibes.

"We left about five in the morning. It was a long night."

At the end, Ed Laughlin of the Ghosts of Georgia team prepared a report about the results of the investigation of the Morton Theatre. "The theater feels great...good energy and no bad vibes at all," said Laughlin.

Electronic Voice Phenomena (EVP) captured by the team that could not be attributed to any of the investigators include the following:

- "I want him out."
- "Mortuary"
- "Good"
- "Yes"
- "Spirit"
- "Hi" or "Hey"

The audio recordings additionally captured whistling, loud unexplained noises, and the sound of footsteps.

When videos recorded during the investigation were reviewed, the following was captured:

- Light anomalies including a blue light like the one reported previously
- A dark mass in one of the auditorium seats where the cold spot has been frequently reported

Investigators also reported batteries draining in equipment suddenly and without explanation.

In a theater office, the team discovered that a file cabinet drawer which was known to be closed earlier had opened on its own. This reportedly happens in the office often. The team set about trying to reproduce a circumstance that might cause the drawer to open. They were unsuccessful.

Ed Laughlin has a warning: "The next time you come to the Morton Theatre, if you hear a whisper in your ear, don't be afraid. It just might be Pink Morton saying 'Hi' to you!"

ATHENS GHOST HUNT: THE MORTON THEATRE, THE VIDEO PRODUCED BY THE ATHENS-CLARKE COUNTY PUBLIC INFORMATION OFFICE ABOUT THE INVESTIGATION, RECEIVED A 2015 NATIONAL SAVVY AWARD FROM THE CITY-COUNTY COMMUNICATIONS & MARKETING ASSOCIATION. CHECK OUT THE VIDEO, PLUS PHOTOS AND MORE INFORMATION ABOUT THE INVESTIGATION AT http://athensclarkecounty.com/6339/Athens-Ghost-Hunt-The-Morton-Theatre.

The Morton Theatre
References

"Athens Ghost Hunt: The Morton Theatre." Athens Ghost Hunt: The Morton Theatre. *Athensclarkecounty.com*. Web. 09 Sept. 2016. <http://athensclarkecounty.com/6339/Athens-Ghost-Hunt-The-Morton-Theatre>.

"Athens Ghost Hunt: The Morton Theatre." YouTube. 2015 National Savvy Award winning video "Athens Ghost Hunt: The Morton Theatre" produced by the Athens-Clarke County Public Information office. *YouTube*, 24 Nov. 2014. Web. 09 Sept. 2016. <https://www.youtube.com/watch?v=yXbM_5jZBlA>.

Aued, Blake. "The Morton Theatre May Be Haunted." *Flagpole Magazine*. 20 Nov. 2014. Web. 09 Sept. 2016.

Clarke, Jeffrey. "Folklore, Facts & Fables Tour"

Davis, Melissa. "Ghosts Among the Kudzu." *DigitalCommons@Kennesaw State University*. Kennesaw State University. Web.

Laughlin, Ed. "Ghosts of Georgia Investigation Report." *Athensclarkecounty.com*. Web. <http://athensclarkecounty.com/DocumentCenter/View/24865>.

"Morton Theatre." Morton Theatre. Web. 09 Sept. 2016. <http://www.mortontheatre.com/history.php>.

Wikipedia contributors. "Morton Theatre." *Wikipedia, The Free Encyclopedia*. 23 Aug. 2016. Web. 9 Sep. 2016.

Author interview with Jeff Montgomery, Athens-Clarke County Public Information Officer

Author interview with a former Morton Theatre employee

THE T.R.R. COBB HOUSE

The T.R.R. Cobb House is a Greek Revival home that was originally built in 1834 at 194 Prince Avenue as a four-over-four Plantation Plain style home. In 1844, the first Chief Justice of the Georgia Supreme Court, Joseph Henry Lumpkin, gave the house as a wedding gift to his daughter Marion and her husband Thomas Reade Rootes Cobb.

In addition to being a lawyer, Tom Cobb was an author, educator, and politician. He advocated the institution of slavery and was an officer in the Confederate army, as well as a staunch supporter of states' rights and Southern Nationalism.

T.R.R. Cobb enlarged the modest home during the late 1840s, and by 1852, had added octagon-shaped wings and a two-story portico with Doric columns.

Thomas Cobb perished in 1862 during the Battle of Fredericksburg during the American Civil War. Following Cobb's death, Marion continued to live in the house until 1873 when she sold it.

After the sale, the house was used as a rental property, fraternity house, and boarding house. The boarding house served meals and most of the tenants were students at the nearby University of Georgia.

In 1962, the Archdiocese of Atlanta purchased the house for use by St. Joseph Catholic Church as a rectory and offices.

In the 1980s, the church planned to demolish the house in pursuit of plans to expand the church. In 1984, the Stone Mountain Memorial Association bought the house and moved the structure to Stone Mountain Park near Atlanta the following year.

The Stone Mountain Memorial Association intended for the house to be restored as a part of a planned "living history village." But, the house sat untouched at Stone Mountain Park for almost two decades after budgetary constraints put plans on indefinite hold.

In 2004, the Watson-Brown Foundation worked with the Georgia Trust for Historic Preservation and the Athens-Clarke Heritage Foundation to purchase the house from the Stone Mountain Memorial Association. It was not until the spring of 2005 that the house was returned to Athens. It now occupies 175 Hill Street in the Cobbham historic district, two blocks from its original location.

The T.R.R. Cobb House underwent a detailed restoration that returned the home to reflect the styles of 1852-1862 when Thomas Cobb was at the peak of his short-lived career. The end result is so spectacular that in 2008, the Georgia Trust awarded the T.R.R. Cobb House its Preservation Award for excellence in restoration.

In 2007, the T.R.R. Cobb House opened to the public as a historic house museum that seeks to cultivate a greater understanding and appreciation of nineteenth-century Southern life.

The house is divided into two exhibition spaces. The lower floor is set up as it would have looked during the period of 1852-1862 and is furnished with original pieces from the Cobb and related families, as well as other Athens families.

The upper floor is more contemporary with changing exhibits and display cases housing original weapons, objects, and documents, including Cobb's Legion artifacts and copies of speeches by T.R.R. and his brother, Howell Cobb.

Because the house has been remodeled over the years, the current configuration is not the way many remember it. When the Catholic church owned it, the place where a stairwell now exists used to be a side entrance and portico.

A priest who formerly occupied the building returned for a visit and told a tale of a close call that nearly destroyed the building. The priests would read the newspaper and then stack them up on the porch. Eventually, they piled up two stacks that went from the floor to the ceiling of the porch. One day, thirty years ago, the pile spontaneously combusted. But miraculously, the fire went out on its own.

After its travels and restoration and that narrow escape from a fiery end, many Athens residents have been able to visit and appreciate the T.R.R. Cobb House. Since the restoration of the home, it is rumored that staff members have heard odd sounds including disembodied footsteps and laughter.

Sam Thomas is the curator of the T.R.R. Cobb House. When I spoke with him, I found out I was not the first one to ask him about strange goings-on in the house.

"We put through about three thousand school kids for tours each year," Mr. Thomas told me. "During October, one of the first questions they all ask is, 'Is this place haunted?'"

Visitors are right to wonder since the resident spooks seem to have a sense of humor about greeting some guests.

Hearing guests arrive at the house is an everyday occurrence. "We hear people coming in because of how heavy the doorknob is," Thomas explained. But, not all arrivals are equal. "It's fairly common that we hear those noises of somebody coming in, but when we go to greet them, no one is there."

Thomas confirmed that the T.R.R. Cobb house often hosts events at night. However, the resident spirits prefer to make their presence known during broad daylight hours.

One employee, an education coordinator named Shannon, had told Thomas about an experience she had in the house.

"Shannon was here late one day on a Saturday. Not long before closing, an older couple came to the door who wanted to tour the house, so she invited them in. The woman asked her, 'Is this place haunted?' Shannon told her, 'We've heard some things during the night but that's about it.' The woman replied, 'Good, because if I walked into a room and saw the chandelier swinging, it would freak me out!'

"The first room on the house tour is the parlor. Shannon said that as soon as they walked into the parlor, the chandelier was swinging. That chandelier was not made to swing, but Shannon had to physically go up there and stop it from swinging.

"In the last ten years, two of the Catholic priests have come back to the house at two different times. Both of them asked me if I had seen the ghost yet."

Thomas indicated that a few nuns that lived in the house at different times had also come back to visit. "The nuns asked if I'd seen the ghost," Thomas said. "According to all them, there is a man in gray that descends the stairs and goes and stands in front of the fireplace mantel. We believe it must be Tom Cobb because he was killed in his Confederate uniform."

One of the front octagonal rooms downstairs is decorated with a portrait of Tom Cobb in his Confederate uniform. This room was Tom Cobb's library. Historians identified the room by the board walls, some of which are visible. Plaster walls would have wicked water up from the ground, but boards kept the books safer.

It was here in the library where Tom Cobb's body lay in state when he was brought home after his death. Though seemingly an ideal place for a ghostly occurrence, the library has no known associated spooky stories. The room next to it is another matter, though.

As Mr. Thomas continued showing me the downstairs of the house, he pointed out one of the antiques furnishing the home. It was a hutch and bookshelf enclosed by glass doors that locked. Thomas informed me that the piece was actually a British piece and didn't truly belong in the house, but it was brought in to hold books that belonged to Tom Cobb's older brother, Howell.

Thomas explained. "It was about eight years ago when I went to put the books into the bookshelf. I tried to get the doors open, but they were locked. In the top drawer, I found a little key, but when I tried it, it didn't work."

Since he didn't have the key, Thomas pulled on the doors with his fingers as best he could, to no avail. "I didn't have anything with me to try to open the doors, so I decided I would use the little key to try to pry them open. Just as I got ready to wedge the key in to try it, the door swung wide open."

"That was kinda weird," Thomas confided.

Lucy Cobb, the oldest daughter, lived in a bedroom upstairs in the home. That room is now an office. Sadly, Lucy died there when she succumbed to scarlet fever at age thirteen. This tragedy could explain why some have seen a little girl peering out of an upstairs window.

"It was about two years ago that a woman told me a story," Thomas said. "She and her daughter were walking down the sidewalk outside. The daughter asked if they could stop in and see the house. The mother replied that since it was Sunday, the house was not open for tours. The little girl replied that they must be open because someone was in there. 'There's a little girl looking at me from the upstairs window,' she told her mother."

Next, Thomas showed me the central hallway in the home. A grand stairway descended in the center and at the bottom stood a tremendous armoire. "This was Tom Cobb's armoire," he informed me.

Thomas opened an inconspicuous panel on one side of the armoire, revealing a coat hook. "This is where he would hang his coat. Sometimes when we come downstairs, this door is wide open. This happens any time of year, even when it is hot and the wood has expanded and you usually have to pry the doors to get them open."

The armoire is not the only creepy part of the stairwell. Thomas related the tale of three women who stopped in one afternoon for a visit. After completing the tour, they were preparing to leave.

"I was standing here at the base of the stairs," Thomas said. "And they were standing next to me. We chatted as they walked. One of the women suddenly asked, 'Who is the woman at the top of the stairs there?' No one was there, so I replied, 'What?' She said 'There's an old black woman standing right there.'" Thomas was shocked as he hadn't mentioned anything about the ghost of the black woman sometimes seen upstairs in the house.

"Supposedly there is an old black woman that looks out of one of the front upstairs windows. The nuns mentioned her, also. We're not sure who that would be, but we do know that some of the slaves lived in the house with the Cobb family."

One story about the T.R.R. Cobb house shows that it's possible ghosts are not immune to modern annoyances.

"We were in here cleaning the piano one day six or seven years ago," Thomas told me. "A fellow came in and wanted to look around the house so we told him, sure, go ahead. Meander around as much as you want.

"He went upstairs to the front rooms above us. We stayed downstairs cleaning the piano. Before long, we heard him talking on his cell phone.

"A few minutes later, he came down and said, 'I'm so sorry!' We asked him what for. He asked, 'Were y'all not just up there?' I said, 'No, we've been down here.'

"When he walked into the octagon upstairs, which was Tom's bedroom, 'I distinctly heard someone behind me saying 'Shhhhhhh!' he told us. And so, I got off the phone. I thought it was y'all telling me to be quiet.'

"He came back about two years later with a friend of his. He took his friend upstairs and was telling him the story. When he started to walk into the bedroom again, his cell phone rang.

"He came downstairs and said to me, 'You'll never believe this. That was my mother that just called me. The last time she called me was when I was right there in that room two years ago.'"

Visit the T.R.R.Cobb house located at 175 hill street to find out what the spirits have in store for you! Hours are Tuesday to Saturday from 10:00am–4:00pm. It is closed on Sundays, Mondays and holidays.

The T.R.R. Cobb House

Portrait of T.R.R. Cobb in his Confederate uniform

Bookcase with Howell Cobb's books that opened by itself

Armoire with coat hook panel that opens on its own

Main stairwell in the T.R.R. Cobb House

The T.R.R. Cobb House
References

Head, Matthew. "Ghosts of Athens, GA (Long but Good!)." *Google Groups*. Newsgroup post. 3 May 1999.

Davis, Melissa. "Ghosts Among the Kudzu." *DigitalCommons@Kennesaw State University*. Kennesaw State University. Web.

Matyka, Doug. "Shadows of the past inhabit the homes of Athens". (Undated and unidentified clipping from the Georgia Ghosts folder in the Hargrett Library collection.)

"Our Story." *Trrcobbhouse.org*. Web. 09 Sept. 2016. <http://www.trrcobbhouse.org/#trrcobbhouse>.

"Visit." *Trrcobbhouse.org*. Web. 09 Sept. 2016. <http://www.trrcobbhouse.org/visit/#visitor-info>.

Wikipedia contributors. "T.R.R. Cobb House." *Wikipedia, The Free Encyclopedia*. 2 Jul. 2016. Web. 9 Sep. 2016.

Author interview with Sam Thomas, Curator of the T.R.R. Cobb House

GRADUATE HOTEL

The buildings now known as the Graduate Hotel in downtown Athens began as the Athens Boiler and Machine Works (or Athens Steam Company), established in 1850 by John Gilleland.

The Athens Steam Company produced cast iron, steam engines, boilers, iron fencing, and more. It was successful until it burned down in 1853 when investors lost everything due to lack of insurance. The fire destroyed a majority of the building, leaving only the interior and exterior brick.

The company reopened in 1854, and in 1856, the famous Arch and iron fencing surrounding the North Campus of the University of Georgia were created there and erected to secure the campus and keep livestock out. The three pillars of the Arch represent the tenets of the Georgia state motto: wisdom, justice, and moderation.

In 1863, the company's name changed to the Athens Foundry and Machine Works. It was at the Foundry that Gilleland built Athens' famous double-barreled cannon for a cost of $350.

The cannon was meant to function by loading both barrels with cannons attached by a chain. By firing both barrels at once, the cannonballs would eject and the attached chain would mow down the advancing enemy. For the rig to work, the powder behind each round shot had to ignite at the same instant, which was impossible.

When tested in 1862, the cannon mowed down trees, tore up a cornfield, knocked down a chimney, and killed an unfortunate cow, none of which was near the intended target. Rumors have claimed that the cannon killed the inventor on the first shot, but Gilleland actually survived, considered the weapon a success, and tried to promote it to the Confederate army, which declined.

After the cannon never functioned as intended, it was eventually presented to the city "...as a memorial of uncertain times. The cannon remains on display at City Hall pointing North, just in case...." (Wikipedia)

The foundry company relocated to Elberton in the 1960s, abandoning the buildings.

In 1973, an Atlanta-based architectural and engineering firm broke ground to develop History Village, intended to be a resort property created from historical buildings and brick remaining after the Foundry fire of 1863.

In 1975, the 19th-century Hoyt House was relocated onto the property and became part of the hotel known as the Hoyt House Country Inn and Tavern. The Hoyt House was originally built in 1829 on a hill in Oglethorpe County. Reverend Nathan Hoyt of Athens purchased the home in 1833 and had it shipped to Athens using a barge on the Oconee River. Between 1833 and 1866, Reverend Hoyt added four rooms and a second floor to the home. Today, the Hoyt House is one of the oldest buildings in Athens-Clarke County.

During the 1970s, the Athens History Village Inn opened and closed numerous times under various ownership. After becoming infamous for seedy activity, it was closed by Athens-Clarke County officials in May of 2000 for "poor management."

In 2001, redevelopment began and the Foundry Park Inn opened, including the Hoyt House restaurant and later adding the Melting Point music venue. In 2014, the hotel reopened as Graduate Athens, converted the Hoyt House to guest suites, and renamed the music venue The Foundry bar. The Graduate Hotel lobby and cafe, music venue, and Foundry bar are all located in the original foundry ironworks buildings.

In the decades-old brick walls of the original Foundry building, today you can still see fingerprints dried in the bricks. These fingerprints were probably left by slave laborers checking the bricks for doneness as they built the buildings.

These fascinating remnants are not all that remains of the past in the buildings that make up the Graduate hotel. It seems a number of previous tenants have chosen to extend their stay.

Local historian Jeff Clarke is a bartender in the Foundry bar at Graduate Hotel. "I've worked here three years and this is a very cool place to work," he told me. "It's got an interesting vibe to it. I've never felt afraid in here, but you get a feeling like you are being watched. Like you are not alone here."

In the Foundry bar area, hotel staff sometimes see a strange man. "I have seen him a few times out of the corner of my eye. He is about my height and has blond or gray hair."

Jeff recounted one such time when he encountered the man late one night. "At the end of the night after a shift, it is usually quiet. You can count up the money from the till and do closing paperwork without distractions.

But one night, I was under the distinct impression that someone was in here with me.

"I was at the bar doing my paperwork and restocking the bar when I heard the door rattle. I looked over, but didn't see anything.

"A few seconds later, I saw some movement out of the corner of my eye. For that split second, I was not alone in here. I saw somebody out of the corner of my eye."

One of the hotel security guards has mentioned to Jeff that he also gets the feeling in the ballroom that there is someone in the room with him. "He comes in and leaves pretty quickly. He times his activities in here to happen while there is someone else present. Then, we all leave together."

Jeff is not sure of the identity of the man that lurks in the ballroom, but he doubts it is tied to the earlier fire at the foundry. "There's no record of anyone dying in the fire here."

If not motivated by a tragic demise, perhaps the spirit has other happier motivations.

"If I were going to haunt someplace, it would be a place like this," Jeff told me enthusiastically. "There's young people here, there's live music, there's activity. That's what I would want to do, watching all the laughing and dancing going on instead of hiding in some musty old building. Haunting this place would be cool."

Jeff is not the only Graduate employee who has confronted the paranormal while on the job. Front desk clerk Laura Deadwyler has had a few hair-raising experiences.

One of Laura's duties is to inspect rooms after they have been cleaned by housekeeping. But, not all inspections are equal.

In particular, she avoids the Hoyt House suites. "I cannot stand going in the top floor of the Hoyt House," she told me.

"A couple of times, when I would go up there to inspect a room, the hair dryer would be plugged in and running. I would shut it off and wonder, 'Who would go off and leave a hair dryer running?' A while later, another employee was doing inspections and came in to find the hair dryer had turned itself back on."

The hair dryer is not the only Hoyt House appliance that seems to have a mind of its own. "The housekeepers claim the television in there will turn on and off by itself," Laura stated.

"I actually got physically sick in there. I don't know why, but that is the last time I went up there. I am so scared of the Hoyt House. I make a point to send someone else to those rooms. I will not go back."

Ghostly activity is not limited to the Hoyt House suites. According to Laura, they also make themselves at home in the Graduate lobby in broad daylight.

"In the lobby, we routinely have to fluff the pillows on the couches. Once, when no one was in the lobby, I fluffed the pillows and set them up like they are supposed to be. Then, I walked back over to the front desk. As soon as I turned back around, the pillows were laying in the middle of the couch."

When not arranging pillows or running hair dryers, the Graduate spooks sometimes head to the kitchen for a snack. Chef Mike has worked in the kitchen for years, both when it was located in the Hoyt House and in its current location in the Foundry building. On more than one occasion, he has encountered the unexplained.

Jeff Clarke readily vouches for Mike's credibility. "I've known Mike for years. He's a no-nonsense guy."

Mike detailed one experience in the Hoyt House kitchen. "I used to work in the Hoyt House early mornings. Most of the time I would open it by myself. So, when I would come on duty, no one was in there. But, when I'd open the door and walk into the kitchen. I'd hear footsteps. Sometimes I would even hear kids' footsteps, like pitter-patter running around. Other times, I have seen a couple of lights turn on and off on their own."

When asked if these occurrences made him feel scared, Mike answered, "Oh, no. It's pretty cool. Every morning, I'd walk in and say, 'Good morning Mr. Hoyt!'"

Mike explained that sometimes a muffled voice emanated from the upstairs but could not be attributed to anyone living. He thought Mr. Hoyt was responsible for the sounds.

"I could never make out what it was saying. I would hear it and go upstairs looking, but nobody was ever there," he said.

His experiences have not made him terrified of the Hoyt House section of the hotel. In fact, quite the opposite. Mike suspects that the renovation to covert the Hoyt House from a kitchen into suites may have gotten the attention of resident ghosts. "I've wanted to rent one of those rooms for a night to see if the construction stirred up more activity."

Despite the interior remodel, the exterior of the Hoyt House looks much the same as it did in 1829. One person who can attest to the fact it has not changed much over the years is Lucy Whitlock.

Lucy Whitlock is 61 years young and has worked on the housekeeping staff at the hotel for the last twelve years. "And I've got twelve grandbabies," she told me proudly.

Lucy was born in 1954 just down the hill from where the Graduate Athens Hotel now stands. She is known to hotel staff as "Miss Lucy." She explained to me her philosophy about people who have passed on.

"I feel like someone be around me sometimes. My peoples like my niece and my older sister. My older sister died from cancer and I was named after her. I can feel sometimes when they around. Ain't nothing scary about it though. They dead, but they right there with ya. It's family.

"This is where I was borned up and raised. See the big train trestle down here?" She pointed down the hill towards the river. "I done ran across that. Me and my brothers. Every trestle around here, we done walked and played on.

"Where the new bus station is—that was our playground. Athens Feed Mill was down there and the coffee company. Used to be a creek back there where they were moonshining back then. That was the good old days, but all that got gone. But, our ball field is still there.

"I grew up in a house on Strong Street that was right across the street [from the Foundry building]. We called this place here the Iron Building.

I used to walk to school every day to College Avenue School. When we got done with school, we were here in this [Foundry] building, playing!

"My Momma used to tell us to stay out of it. It was sort of haunted, in a way. She'd say 'Them dead folks is gonna git you.' But, we didn't pay it too much attention because we was young. We said, 'Well, they gotta catch us first!'

"We was just rough and tough kids, playing in the building we weren't supposed to be in. I was 11 or 12 years old. Me and my five brothers, we messed around playing in here all the time. We heard a lot of noise and stuff but we just kept on playing. We was having fun."

According to Miss Lucy, it was common knowledge back then for people in the neighborhood that the Foundry buildings were haunted.

"It stayed a little haunted on this area. People would never come in the building. All the windows were broken out. You wouldn't even walk in the driveway. We didn't see no peoples over here. People were scared to come through here. Everybody said it was haunted."

"People used to work in here during slavery times and had iron chains wrapped around their legs and hands. Playing in here, we could see where they left that stuff on the walls. We'd see the big iron chains where they were chained up by their ankles and wrists. There was a lot of weird stuff in here. A lot of slaves died in here."

Despite the grisly surroundings, Lucy and her siblings frequented the building to play. Sometimes, it seemed they were not alone.

"We would hear chains rattling. You would hear people hitting on the wall. You would hear voices say, 'Let me out! Let me out!" They could have been standing right beside us. We could feel something.

"We'd go back and tell Momma that we heard voices, people hollering and screaming. She'd say, 'I told you it was haunted! I told y'all to stay out of there!' Lucy smiled. "But we were trying to find a treasure."

Jeff Clarke brought in an old picture of the Foundry buildings. He showed it to Lucy and asked if that was how she remembered it.

"Oh, yeah. Back then, it didn't have no windows or nothing in it."

"There was another building down the road that we called the Old Warehouse. They used to sell tools out of it. It was next to where the *Athens Banner-Herald* office is now. They've made apartments out of that building. Me and my brothers are like, 'Nuh uh, not us!' Folks used to say there were bodies were buried in the walls there. During the remodel when they made apartments out of it, they found bones. It's haunted, too."

Lucy had a living connection with the history of the location as well. She used to rent an apartment in town from Mr. Hoyt's great-grandson. Apparently, he used the connection to check up on family members.

"He'd ask me, 'Miss Lucy, you ain't heard nothing up there have you? My granddaddy ain't making noise, is he?' I told him I just go in to clean the room and say, 'Mr. Hoyt, if you're in here, I need some help!" She laughs. "You can help me make this bed!"

Kidding aside, Lucy has a method for avoiding being creeped out on the job.

"I mostly don't like telling people stories about this place. If I do, I'll get scared and then I don't want to go in that room and work. So, I just keep it to myself."

Lucy did eventually find the courage to tell me a few stories about strange events in the hotel. She explained that at night the housekeepers would line up the carts in a storage room. But, when they came in the next morning, all the carts would be thrown up against the wall, even though no one had been in there.

She also recalled an incident when the Hoyt House was used as a kitchen and restaurant. "Two guys who worked at that kitchen came running out of the Hoyt House at a hundred miles an hour! I said, 'What's wrong with you?' He told me, 'I went up there and the pots and stuff were rattling around! I had to go! I didn't even get the stuff I needed!'"

One guest room that Miss Lucy did not care for in particular was Room 119. She and another woman on the housekeeping staff regularly had bad experiences when they cleaned the room.

"There was a woman who worked here called Mrs. L. who swore that Room 119 is haunted," Miss Lucy said. "She was constantly telling us 'Don't go in Room 119! I don't want that room no more! Let somebody else clean it!' She swore that something was in that room.

"She'd say, 'Miss Lucy, I can't never get out of that room.' I'd say, 'Why not?' Mrs. L said it took the longest time to clean that room. 'I go to sweating and it's like there's something holding me in there. Like it's keeping me in the room and don't want me to leave.'"

"I believe her," Miss Lucy said. "It shouldn't take no hour to do that room and it shouldn't happen to her all the time. But every other day or so she had that room and it happened to her. It didn't happen in any of the other rooms. Just that one room.

"You can feel when somebody is next to you. You can feel somebody looking at you. If she feel it, she feel it."

Eventually Mrs. L. refused to go back in to the room and they had to get Miss Lucy to clean it.

"I noticed in there, on the left-hand side, on the wall by the window, there's a spot in the corner that is a big circle with a smaller circle inside of it. That spot won't go away. No matter how many times you paint it, it comes back.

"Mrs. L. told Miss Lucy, 'Maurice painted this room three times for me because I was scared, but that spot just keeps showing back up through the paint!' A week later, she would say, 'Come look! It done come back again!'

"I think it's still there," Miss Lucy said.

The spirit in Room 119 is not shy about making its presence known, both inside the room and outside, as Miss Lucy related. "A lady I know says you can drive by the hotel late at night, three o'clock in the morning. Ain't nobody in the rooms and every light can be off downstairs, but that one light will be on in the very last room on the bottom in the corner. That's 119. Lots of people say that. Take a notice one night when you come up that road early in the morning."

Laura Deadwyler agrees that something is odd about 119.

She informed me that Room 119 always causes phone trouble at the front desk. It lights up like a call is coming from that room, but no one is booked in 119 or staying in that room. This happened so often that they removed the phone entirely from the room. Afterward, everyone was floored when lights for calls from Room 119 still happened.

"People staying in that room commonly want to change rooms," Laura said.

Miss Lucy's family ties to the location are as diverse as well. Her niece worked at the hotel back when it was called History Village. "She said a lady got killed back then in the hall by Room 225," Lucy said. "They don't know if she was murdered or killed herself, but she died.

"For four years, I used to be on that back hall by myself doing double beds. I know nobody was back there because everything was empty. I'd walk down through there to get my cart and when I got to 225, somebody was singing.

"I thought somebody left the TV on in the room. Sometimes, when somebody is cleaning and takes their lunch break, they'll sit with the TV on. But, I'm like, 'Wait a minute! Ain't nobody supposed to be in these rooms!' I had my key and opened the door.

"That room was just as clean...no TV on, no radio. I shut the door back and went around and got my cart. I went on down through there to do the rooms on that side and then I heard the singing again! I said, 'Somebody is singing.'"

"I started opening doors to check for a TV left on, all the way from 220 to 225. When I got to 225 and opened the door, they stopped singing.

"I shut the door back and eased on around with my cart. Then, I thought, 'I don't think I'm going back to put the cart up!' Because every time I started around, you could hear somebody singing. She could have been standing there looking right at me.

"I shut the door up, came back around the corner to do my room at 234. They were singing again. I don't know who it was."

If you are feeling brave, check in to the Graduate Hotel at 295 East Dougherty Street and see what the spirits have in store for you.

The Foundry buildings approximately during the 1960s.
Photo courtesy of Jeff Clarke

Graduate Hotel lobby in the Foundry building

The Hoyt House at Graduate Hotel

Fingerprints in the brick at the Foundry building

Graduate Hotel References

"Athens Boiler and Machine Works Records, 1934-1986." *Southern Historical Collection at the Louis Round Wilson Library*. Records #4932, Southern Historical Collection, Wilson Library, University of North Carolina at Chapel Hill.

Athens-Clarke Heritage Room. "5 March 1901: Athens Foundry and Machine Works "Now Running At Full Blast"" This Day in Athens: Athens-Clarke County Heritage Room. Web. 09 Sept. 2016.

"History and Timeline." Handout provided by Graduate Athens

Wikipedia contributors. "Double-barreled cannon." Wikipedia, The Free Encyclopedia. Wikipedia, The Free Encyclopedia, 25 May. 2016. Web. 9 Sep. 2016.

Author interview with Historian Jeff Clarke

Author interview with Graduate Hotel employee Lucy Whitlock

Author interview with Graduate Hotel employee Laura Deadwyler

Author interview with Graduate Hotel employee Michael Southwick

FIRE HALL NUMBER ONE

Athens Fire Hall Number One has safeguarded downtown Athens since it was built in 1912 on its hilltop location on North Thomas Street overlooking the North Oconee River.

Originally, the fire hall was scheduled to be built in 1913, but the fire chief lobbied to move up the timeline in order to avoid beginning occupation during the year with the unlucky "13." Luck was with them and Athens city engineer Captain J.W. Barnett was able to design and build the hall during 1912. The fire hall was designed in the Craftsman architectural style and was opened for occupation before the start of the new year. One of the first professional fire departments in the country, the Athens brigade was equipped with horse-drawn fire wagons and one motorized vehicle.

At that time, streets in downtown Athens were created with old cobblestones originally used as ballast for ships coming into and out of Savannah. Years later, both sides of the old Fire Hall retained cobblestone from alleyways suggesting that the hall had originally been built in the middle of the street. Later, during construction of the Classic Center, some of these original cobblestones were preserved and used in the parking lot as decoration.

Fire Hall Number One served the community through the late 1970s. In 1979, a new station was built down the street near the Ware-Lyndon House and the company relocated there.

After the firemen moved out, the Athens Area Chamber of Commerce moved in, using the building as their headquarters until the late 1980s. At that time, Athens city commissioners considered incorporating the Fire Hall as part of a proposed new performing arts center. This proposal prompted heated debates about the Classic Center design that continued throughout the early 1990s. One of the architects on the job was adamant that it was impossible to incorporate the Fire Hall into the Classic Center design. Many locals suggested that the hall instead be moved to a new location or just torn down.

But, the citizens of Athens rallied to save the historic building. Eventually, architect Rabun Hatch developed plans that included the old Fire Hall and the plans were approved. During construction, Fire Hall Number One was thoroughly remodeled. It is now the centerpiece of the design and serves as the box office for the Classic Center, which was completed in 1996.

Fortunately, the remodel did salvage some aspects of the old fire hall. Original pine wood flooring was refinished and preserved. The floors are unique in that the boards of the floor are turned on their sides to provide extra support for weight of the fire wagons and horses. Horses anxious to pull wagons pawed the floors and left deep gouges behind.

The high windows above the stable floor accommodated room for tools and tack required by firefighters, a room now converted for meetings. Originally, three brass fire poles connected living areas on the second story to the lower stable area. The upper rooms are now executive office space, including the one remaining brass pole still intact. The outer doors of the

Fire Hall were remodeled to resemble the original glass doors which were removed to build an elevator.

The Classic Center is fortunate to have an original buggy that was donated to the fire department in 1901 by the Southern Mutual Insurance Company, so the fire chief would not have to ride on horseback. The buggy is displayed parked on the original pine wood floors, just as it had when it served the department decades ago.

Captain Hiram Peeler had a distinguished career with the Athens Fire Department as a member for over a quarter century. Born in Clarke County on November 25, 1861, Hiram Peeler joined the volunteer department in 1881 and became a paid member in January 1891. He eventually became a captain and served until his death at 7:50 p.m. on Wednesday, Feb. 24, 1926.

Captain Peeler died at a local hospital from injuries received while on duty when he fell down an elevator shaft fighting a fire at McDorman-Bridges Funeral Home. At that time, Captain Peeler was the oldest member of the Athens Fire Department, both in time of service and in age.

Captain Peeler was buried in Oconee Hill Cemetery, but it seems he still prefers to occupy his former place of employment. Rumors suggest that after Captain Peeler's death, strange activities occurred in Fire Hall Number One while it still served as a firehouse and during its time housing the Athens Area Chamber of Commerce. Many believe that his spirit makes its presence known in the Classic Center building to this day.

The Athens Area Chamber of Commerce moved in to occupy Fire Hall Number One during the early 1980s. Soon after settling in, employees were unsettled by events they could not explain. They consulted members of the fire department who had recently vacated the building to see if they had had similar experiences. As Phil Sanderlin describes in his *Athens Observer* article, the firemen and Chamber employees all had tales to tell:

Secretary Gale Scarborough laughed when a fireman told her that when the Chamber of Commerce moved into the old fire hall, they got the spirit of a former firefighter with the building. She's not superstitious, she said, but she's not too sure now either.

"Just this past Monday," she said, "I was sitting here at the desk when I heard a cabinet door open and close. It makes a distinctive sound. I thought someone was in there who hadn't bothered to check back in, but when I got up and looked, the room was empty. I've heard a door slam and footsteps when nobody was there. I can't explain it."

Older members of the Clarke County Fire Department can offer an explanation. The building, they say, houses the ghost of Captain Otis Peeler, a former fireman who's been heard by many members of the fire department, including Fire Chief Jimmy Hansford.

"Mr. Peeler was a fireman for many years," Hansford said. "He worked his way up through the ranks and became Captain Peeler.

He was assistant chief before he retired. He retired back in the early '60s. He died shortly afterward. He was accused of coming back and 'living' in the basement area and bedroom area of the station. A lot of men have heard footsteps and the kitchen door creaking late at night when there was no one there, and all the doors were locked. I really thought I heard someone on the stairs one night, and I wasn't the only person who heard it."

Paul Miller, economic development director for the chamber, reports two incidents within the last month while he was alone in the building.

"One Saturday night I finished some work and went into the boardroom to watch some TV," Miller said. "There was this horror movie on, and I swear I heard someone walking upstairs. There's just storage space up there, and it's kept locked. I got up and went home. "That was two weeks ago. I was here last Sunday afternoon, and there was the same situation in the boardroom. I heard someone walking upstairs again."

Scarborough related that another woman who works at the chamber not only heard footsteps, but felt a hand on her shoulder: "She came in and told me, 'I don't mind him walking around, but I don't want him touching me.' I don't believe in things like this, but I wonder."

Chamber of Commerce Executive Vice President Allen Stephenson is the calm, business-like type not inclined to believe in ghosts. He is puzzled about the chain swinging, though.

"I don't know what caused it," Stephenson said. "There's a chain hanging from the roof in the basement. It's where they used to suspend the chief's buggy. I walked down there and the chain was swinging back and forth, not just a little motion, but very noticeably. None of the staff had been down there, and when I checked the outside door, no one was out in the driveway."

Assistant Fire Chief Wendell Faulkner was not surprised at Stephenson's experience. "He used to rattle that chain all the time," Faulkner said. "A lot of people heard him. One night when I was on night duty and up at 3 a.m., I heard the screen door in the kitchen slam and heard someone walking toward the stove and sink area. I stepped out of the dispatching room and jumped up on the water wagon part of the truck and looked into the window. Nobody was in there. "No one believes that the late Captain Peeler is "haunting" the old fire station to scare folks. The firemen believe he was just too dedicated a member of the department to want to leave the building where he spent so many years serving the public.

Whatever is causing the footsteps and other sounds, of a spirit origin or not, Allen Stephenson vowed it would not interfere with the business of the Athens-Clarke County Chamber of Commerce. "I hope he's a friendly ghost," said Stephenson. "Perhaps he inspires us to do even better work."

For more than a decade, the Classic Center has been home to the Athens Convention and Visitors Bureau (CVB) and has been a community venue. A local researcher for the Athens-Clarke Heritage Foundation (Mrs. R.) spoke with employees of the Athens Chamber of Commerce who worked for the CVB located in Fire Hall Number One.

All employees at the Classic Center and CVB were familiar with Captain Peeler's story and rumors about his ghost. Mrs. R. is convinced that "...some employees are sure in their hearts and in their minds that Captain Peeler remains in their midst at the fire hall."

CVB employees have described papers that would rustle or fly off their desk when no draft was present. They witnessed drawers opening and closing seemingly of their own accord with no one nearby. Sometimes, when alone in a room, they experienced a strong feeling of another presence. "They would experience someone being in the room with them. But, they never actually saw him and they couldn't explain it. It was just weird stuff they couldn't explain that they would attribute it to him," the researcher described.

One employee left the building to go to lunch. Upon her return, she approached the building from the walkway crossing Foundry Street. She could clearly see into the Chamber of Commerce. The woman was surprised to see an older man inside the office wearing a dark, fireman-type uniform. Immediately, the woman recalled the stories that co-workers had told about Captain Peeler. She was very excited.

"She wondered, 'Who is this?' and ran across the street and into the building," Mrs. R. reported. "She asked everyone she ran into if they had just seen someone wearing a uniform walking around. Each person replied that they had not. The woman looked and looked. After an exhaustive search, she was excited and happy because she was pretty sure that she had seen the ghost of Captain Peeler."

Mrs. R. relates another tale dating back more than a decade. A former security guard at the Classic Center was making his rounds, closing up and securing all the doors. "At that time, Captain Peeler's fire wagon was on display downstairs in the old fire hall. The guard was making his rounds and as he turned a corner, he saw a person in a dark uniform standing beside the fire wagon. The guard turned to walk away, but then processed what he had seen. He realized that he shouldn't expect to see a man in uniform standing by the wagon at that time. He turned back around to address the person and find out who he was. But when he looked, the man was gone. Later, he told people that he did believe that he had seen Captain Peeler's apparition."

In 2012, Mrs. R. had an experience of her own at the old Fire Hall Number One. A visitor made arrangements to investigate the fire hall to capture evidence of a haunting by Captain Peeler's ghost, and Mrs. R. joined her.

The visiting lady had electromagnetic field (EMF) meters and other investigative apparatuses. Mrs. R., the lady, and the lady's thirteen-year-old daughter met with a Classic Center employee at the building and set up in a conference room. While Mrs. R., the Classic Center employee, and the lady were all on one side of the conference room, the daughter was on the other side of the room holding an EMF detector.

The lady would address Captain Peeler out loud, asking questions while the daughter monitored the EMF detector for results. Suddenly, the EMF detector began beeping wildly. This is an indication of an electrical source that some believe indicates a ghostly presence. If so, the presence was right beside the daughter. The mother continued to ask questions and the EMF meter continued to beep shrilly. Then, the daughter started rubbing her eyes which had begun to bother her. Mrs. R. wondered if they should stop the investigation to find out what was wrong with the girl's eyes, but they kept going. The Classic Center employee crossed the room and stood beside the daughter.

According to Mrs. R., after the investigation was completed, the Classic Center employee confessed, "When I moved and stood next to the daughter, my eyes started hurting, too. It was like smoke was being blown in them."

"Yes!" The daughter agreed. "That's what it was like! I couldn't figure out why my eyes were stinging and hurting. But, it was like there was smoke." Mrs. R. believes this incident was related to Captain Peeler being a firefighter. She told me, "His way of relating his identity was to have them experience the smoke that was his nemesis for so many years."

The Classic Center is located at 300 North Thomas Street in downtown Athens.

Fire Hall Number One
References

Davis, Melissa. "Ghosts Among the Kudzu." *DigitalCommons@Kennesaw State University*. Kennesaw State University. Web.

Head, Matthew. "Ghosts of Athens, GA (Long but Good!)." *Google Groups*. Newsgroup post. 3 May 1999.

Lee, Sarah. "Classic Places: Fire Hall Anchors Classic Center." *Onlineathens.com*. *Athens Banner-Herald*, 5 Jan. 2000. Web.

Peeler, Edwin. "Hirman H Peeler." *Genealogy.com*. 20 July 2012. Web. 09 Sept. 2016.

Sanderlin, Phil. "Staff: Ghost roams C of C." *The Athens Observer*. June 14, 1984. (Clipping from the Georgia Ghosts folder in the Hargrett Library collection.)

Author interview with a local researcher for the Athens-Clarke Heritage Foundation.

THE WARE-LYNDON HOUSE

Dr. Edward Rowell Ware first moved to Athens in 1829 to practice medicine. He was one of Athens' most prominent physicians, practicing during the antebellum, Civil War, and post-Civil War periods.

During the 1840s, Dr. Ware built a two-story, classic Greek Revival house at 293 Hoyt Street in the fashionable Lickskillet neighborhood of Athens. In the mid-1850s, the Wares remodeled the house to reflect an Italianate style, including additions such as marble mantles, ornate plasterwork, and gas lighting. On the outside, brackets under the eaves and intricate ironwork were added.

Mr. and Mrs. Ware hosted lavish parties attended by the likes of William Hope Hull, who founded the University of Georgia's law school in 1859. The Ware home was described as "one of the centers of social life in Athens." Some say that the character of Dr. Meade in Margaret Mitchell's *Gone with the Wind* was based on Dr. Ware.

In 1848, Dr. Ware was elected the first mayor of Athens and served four consecutive one-year terms. During the Civil War, Dr. Ware served in the Thunderbolts, the Athens Home Guard that helped protect Athens. The war left the home untouched and Dr. Ware lived there until his death in 1873.

In 1878, the home was purchased from the Ware heirs by another physician who had served in the Civil War, Edward S. Lyndon. After suffering a breakdown from performing amputations during the war, Lyndon made his living as a druggist. Lyndon remodeled the home again, installing Victorian murals, as well as stenciling and grain-painted finishes on the woodwork, walls and ceilings. Many of these features remain intact in the dining room of the home to this day.

Lyndon lived in the home until his death in 1917. In 1920, the Lyndon heirs removed many of the original architectural elements from the house and built a new home in Washington, Georgia. Afterward, the building was a rental property until 1938.

The City of Athens bought the Ware-Lyndon house in 1939. This made the Ware-Lyndon house the second city-owned building after City Hall. During World War II, it was the headquarters for the U.S.O. After the war, it housed government offices, including the Veterans Administration, Red Cross, and Labor Department. The house became headquarters for the newly formed City of Athens Recreation Department during the 1950s and was used for community youth programs, dances and social gatherings.

The city completed a major restoration on the Ware-Lyndon house in 1960, during which time the out-buildings were removed. The facility became an Athens Recreation Department center and during the 1970s, the home hosted dance classes and Cub Scout troop meetings. The Ware-Lyndon House was placed on the National Register of Historic Places in 1976.

In 1973, the downstairs of the Ware-Lyndon house was used as an art gallery and the upstairs for art classes. The Lyndon House Arts Center was one of the most successful art centers in Georgia and gained national recognition. The home hosted art group meetings, festivals, and special events.

During the 1980s and 1990s, enrollment for popular programs at the Lyndon House Arts Center exceeded capacity. In 1994, a $6-million-dollar budget was approved to restore the historic house and expand the arts center. In May of 1999, the 38,000-square-foot expansion adjoining the original structure opened to the public. It contains galleries, studios, classrooms, and offices and is operated by the Athens-Clarke County Department of Leisure Services. The original Ware-Lyndon House was renovated as a period house museum.

Dr. Ware is not letting his death in 1873 stop him from continuing to make appearances, according to many witnesses. A man wearing a black suit is sometimes seen on the landing of the grand stairway in the entrance of the home, even when no one has been allowed inside.

Some attribute the mystery man's appearance to another historical source. Lonnie Spaulding and his pregnant wife, Nellie, were visiting from Sapelo Island, Georgia and staying at the Lyndon House. The day arrived when Nellie went into labor. But, at that time, Lonnie was in town conducting business. Lonnie was told of his wife's condition and summoned back to the house for the delivery of the child. While distracted and hurrying to the house, Lonnie stepped into the street and was struck by a passing horse-drawn wagon. He was killed instantly.

Some suspect that the man seen by staff and guests who appears on the stairs is Lonnie Spaulding. He appears to be finely dressed and pacing nervously back and forth, checking his pocket watch, as if waiting for the news of the birth of his child.

I spoke with Mrs. L., who is very familiar with the Ware-Lyndon house. She lived near the house and her children walked down the street after school to do arts and crafts at the Lyndon House Arts Center. She also worked as the first costumed docent for Lyndon House and gave tours to people who visited. She handcrafted her own historic clothing and 1860s dresses.

One day, Mrs. L. was wearing her costume and waiting for a tour group to come through the house. "There's a large hall that runs from the front door straight into the dining room, and on the back wall, there is a huge beautiful mirror," Mrs. L. told me. The mirror tilts down, so she could use it to check her costume and make sure her petticoats weren't showing. As she checked her outfit, she noticed in the mirror that there was someone standing behind her.

Mrs. L. wasn't startled because there were a number of people in the house, such as people who work upstairs. But, this was a tall man wearing what looked like a 19th-century outfit. When Mrs. L. turned around to speak to him, was no one there.

She laughed about it to herself and did not immediately assume she had seen a ghost. "He was not filmy or translucent. He looked like a solid person," she told me. Upon mentioning it to other people who worked at the house, some admitted that they had also seen the man.

Mrs. L. is not sure who the man might be, but theorizes that he is someone historically associated with the house.

"The area where I saw him used to be the butler's pantry, where the cooks would bring the food out from the kitchen. It would be prepared and finalized before being served to the family in the dining room."

"I don't scare easily," she told me, "but a number of times when I was the only one in the house, I would sense that I was not alone."

Another Athens-Clarke County employee often came to the Lyndon House Arts Center for meetings. During the Spring of 2010, she was to go there and meet her new boss. "It was my first meeting with him and I had never been there before. I wasn't sure where to go, so, I went around to the front door of the historic house thinking that that was the way you would enter. I rang the doorbell. It rang and rang. And, I waited and I waited."

She looked through the glass of the front door to see if anyone was coming to greet her. "Then, I saw this man come down to the first level of the stairs. He looked down at me."

"What I noted about him was that he had on this very formal black suit. And, it was really hot out. One of these really hot Southern days. At first, I thought it was my boss and I wondered if maybe he was going to a wedding or something. I thought, 'He's really gonna be hot in that.' And, it was one of those old-fashioned things, you know, with the white collar and the real thin tie? A long suit. So, that was really weird. And, he kept staring at me. He kept walking back and forth and looking down."

According to her, this went on for a couple of minutes.

"I'm thinking, 'Are you gonna come down and open the door?'" she told me. "He went back upstairs and disappeared. Then, he came back down and was staring. It was really strange. I said to myself 'What is his problem?' Then, he left and didn't come back. I stood there for a while and I thought, 'Jesus.'

"I walked around to the modern part of the building and found an unlocked door. I went in and there is my boss standing there in a red shirt and khaki pants. I said, 'Oh, you're here! What's with that guy in the black suit?' He said 'What guy in the black suit? I'm the only one here.'

"It was only him and one other person at Reception. He said, 'You saw the man in the black suit?' I said, 'Yeah!' He said, 'Oh, my God, he has been seen by people periodically for years going way back. It's a real honor to be able to see the man in the black suit.' But, he wasn't really there."

"Then we went [to the historic house] for a meeting and there was nobody over there. That really creeped me out."

"At the time, it never occurred to me that that would have been something weird. He looked like a regular person."

"I was so curious to find out who this guy was, I went in to the historic house and began looking at some of the photos. I didn't find a photo of somebody that really looked exactly like him. He seemed kind of young. My boss was about 40 and the man looked about that age. He wasn't like an old man with gray hair or something like that. But, I did see pictures of that suit. It definitely was a period suit. I thought that when I saw it, which is why I thought of a wedding, because it wasn't the kind of suit that one would wear to a meeting. It was formal, the way they used to have with the long coat."

The man in black is not the only departed resident seen in the home.

"There have been stories of people seeing a woman in the house," she told me. "From outside, they look up and see a face in the window. In fact, from what I understand, seeing the woman is more common than seeing the man in black."

She does not take every anecdote at face value, however.

"A lot of people say things happen. Like, recently some workers in the new part of the building said that a chair flew across the floor and that other creepy things have happened. I'm pretty skeptical."

Eventually, her own office was located in the Ware-Lyndon house. "You hear a lot of sounds in the historic house, where my office was. You do hear what you think is somebody coming up the stairs. You walk out and say 'Helllloooooooo?' and nobody is there. I'd be in my office by myself early in the morning and hear stuff like doors slamming. So, you go down and you walk through both buildings and nobody is there."

"There is also a security camera that would go off and we would check it. We'd see some kind of light, but it could be dust. We always hoped that we would see something. But, unfortunately, we never did."

Regarding her sighting of the man in black, her skepticism extends only so far. "It's sort of bizarre. I have no idea."

The historic Ware-Lyndon House is open for tours. It is closed on Sundays and UGA home football game Saturdays.

The Ware-Lyndon House

The Ware-Lyndon House
References

Clarke, Jeffrey. "Folklore, Facts & Fables Tour"

Wikipedia contributors. "Ware-Lyndon House." *Wikipedia, The Free Encyclopedia.* Wikipedia. 2 Jul. 2016. Web. 9 Sep. 2016.

Hammes, Mary Jessica. "Holidays and History." *Online Athens. Athens Banner-Herald.* 13 Dec. 2001. Web. 09 Sept. 2016.

"Historic Ware-Lyndon House." The Athens-Clarke Heritage Foundation. Athens-Clarke Heritage Foundation. Web. 09 Sept. 2016.

Author interview with a long time Athens resident

Author interview with Historian Jeff Clarke

Author interview with a former Lyndon House employee

THE TAYLOR-GRADY HOUSE

The Taylor-Grady House is a Greek Revival house located at 634 Prince Avenue near downtown Athens. A gallery wraps the exterior of the Taylor-Grady House on three sides, supported by thirteen massive fluted Doric columns.

It was originally built in 1844 by General Robert Taylor, who immigrated to Savannah from Ireland in the 1790s as a teen-ager, later becoming a wealthy cotton merchant and leader of the Georgia state militia. It was a summer home until his sons enrolled in the University of Georgia, after which the family occupied the home full time.

In 1863, the house was purchased from the Taylor family by Major William S. Grady while he was on furlough from the Confederate Army. Major Grady returned to the war and, sadly, was killed at the Battle of Petersburg in Virginia.

Major Grady's son, Henry Grady, was born in Athens in 1850. He lived at the Taylor-Grady House with his mother, Anne, while attending the University of Georgia from 1865 until 1868 when he graduated.

Henry once referred to the house as "an old southern home, with its lofty pillars, and its white pigeons fluttering down through the golden air." His family occupied the home until 1872.

Henry Grady eventually became the managing editor of the Atlanta Constitution. In 1886, Grady gave a widely reprinted speech at the New England club in New York City. Known as the "New South" speech, it urged harmonious relations between Northern and Southern states. In that speech, he stated, "There was a South of slavery and secession; that South is dead. A South of union and freedom; that South, thank God, is living, breathing, growing every hour."

The speech was well received by listeners and during the Reconstruction Era that followed the American Civil War, Grady was a leading force in the reintegration of the American South.

Henry Grady died in Atlanta at the age of 39 of pneumonia. The Taylor-Grady House is the only known surviving home of Henry W. Grady.

In 1890, the attached kitchen and rear sleeping porch were added to the house. In 1917, electricity and plumbing were added. During the 1950s, a dance studio opened, but did not last. The home then stood vacant for thirteen years, often vandalized and looted.

In 1966, the Taylor-Grady House was purchased by the City of Athens and after negotiations, leased to the Athens Junior Assembly in 1968. After extensive renovation, the house was included in the 1969 Spring Tour of Homes. The restoration included installing air conditioning, upgrading the kitchen, and remodeling the main rooms. A consignment shop operated inside below the kitchen, while the outside saw the addition of a patio and brick walkways. The Junior Ladies Garden Club executed a landscape plan from the UGA School of Environmental Design.

The Taylor-Grady House

The Taylor-Grady House was declared a National Historic Landmark in 1976. It is now a historic house museum maintained by the Junior League of Athens and retains some original woodwork, plaster, and fireplace mantels.

Rich in history, the Taylor-Grady House has sheltered families who have suffered several tragic deaths. Some believe this is cause for the house to be haunted.

In 1859, General Taylor's legs were almost completely severed in a horrific accident when he was slow to get off a train. He died three days later. His son, Richard, received the house as a wedding gift, but did not enjoy it long. His wife died very young and is reputed to be seen wandering the halls, looking for her groom.

When Major William S. Grady was killed at the Battle of Petersburg, his son Henry twice reported seeing a hazy vision at the top of the stairs, as well as the sound of footsteps running down the stairs. Henry attributed these occurrences to his deceased father.

As the headquarters of the Junior League of Athens, the Taylor-Grady House is currently the site of many weddings and other celebrations. Some of these parties are more memorable than others.

On November 30, 1991, a woman and two fellow Junior League members were leaving the Taylor-Grady House just before midnight. It happened that there was not an event in progress at the house that night. Or, so they believed.

As they walked through the main floor, they felt the presence of a party attended by a large number of people. The women even smelled liquor as if the party goers stood just next to them. Since that experience, the woman refuses to be inside the house alone.

Also, a Confederate soldier is rumored to make an appearance during the Christmas season at Taylor-Grady. When I spoke with Elizabeth Elliott,

Administrative Director and Event Coordinator at the Taylor-Grady House, she informed me that she had not seen him.

Since the Taylor-Grady House hosts numerous events, one of my first questions to Elizabeth was whether at any time, an event was going on and there was a disruption due to a strange event or occurrence. Elizabeth did not know of any.

She explained that events take place mostly outside. What does go on inside is piecemeal and no one stays inside for an extended time, which might make it harder for anyone to notice if something did happen. Also, no one attending events stays in the house overnight, so there are not many people to witness any strange nocturnal events.

Elizabeth relates the most recent paranormal event that has taken place at the Taylor-Grady House occurred in the early 1980s.

A former Junior League president had a young daughter who was around seven years old and she would often bring her daughter with her when she worked there.

"The daughter would hang around at the house and play while she worked," Elizabeth reported. Usually, the daughter stayed close to her mother. She would find projects for the daughter since she commonly was bored.

"One time, the daughter went upstairs at the house on her own. Soon, the mom heard the daughter making a ruckus upstairs playing. She was glad that he daughter had found something to entertain herself for a change.

"After a long while, the mom was impressed that the daughter had found something to amuse herself for that much time. But, it was getting late. The mom called up the stairs to tell the daughter it was time to leave. The daughter yelled downstairs and said she didn't want to leave yet. Surprised, the mom insisted and told her to come on downstairs.

"When the daughter finally came downstairs, her mom asked her, 'What were you doing up there?' The daughter answered, 'Oh, I was playing with the other little girl.'

The mom was startled because she knew there was no other little girl in the house and had not been all day. But, the daughter insisted that there was another little girl and mentioned that she had worn a costume of old fashioned clothes."

The Taylor-Grady House employs residence managers who live on site as caretakers for the building. These residence managers are typically the only people to stay overnight and spend the most time alone in the house.

During the 1980s, a man and his wife stayed in the Taylor-Grady House as residence managers. They visited the house when Elizabeth was first hired and they asked her if she'd had any encounters yet. Elizabeth replied a surprised, "No! Did you have encounters?"

"Oh, yeah!" they answered.

The couple told Elizabeth about a model ship that was displayed in a glass case upstairs in the center hallway. The woman told Elizabeth that, as she cleaned, she could feel someone's eyes on her, watching. "Every single time I was cleaning the glass on the case, I always felt like there was somebody behind me." Not just a creepy feeling, Elizabeth elaborated, but, a presence of someone standing behind her and feeling a breath on her neck. "And, every single time, I had to turn around and check. But, when I turned around, there was never anyone there."

The woman knew there was nothing at that location in the hall that could create a draft that would trick her. The episodes remained a creepy mystery.

After hearing that story, Elizabeth was always wary in the hallway upstairs and kept a nervous eye on the ship. "The ship is still in the house upstairs, but it has been moved out of the hallway into another room," she said.

The woman's husband had strange experiences, too, during their time as residence managers. But, most he could explain away as being a shadow or play of light or something else that seemed a logical explanation. This he was glad for, since he was a logical kind of fellow by nature. Only once did something happen that he had no logical explanation for, as Elizabeth related.

"He was lying in bed one night after he woke up. At first, he wasn't sure what had awakened him. But, then he was hit in the face with a smell. It was a strong, old fashioned perfume. It was a lilac scent so strong that it woke him up and made him nauseous. He couldn't breathe.

"The smell affected him so badly that he had to leave the room to get a breath of fresh air. He stepped outside the room for about thirty seconds. When he went back into the room, he was amazed to find that the smell was completely gone. There was no trace of it."

This was the only event that made him question whether there was really something paranormal going on in the house. He asserted that the experience had to be something unusual because there was no logical explanation for it.

Elizabeth also spoke of a woman in black who supposedly haunts the house. Several different people have told her about a woman in all black who appears to people upstairs in the house. People with no prior knowledge of the story of the woman in black will offer in conversation that they think they "saw something" and describe the woman in black.

Various people who have spent time at the Taylor-Grady House as Junior League members, doing work on the house, or attending events have all asked her, "Have you seen her yet?"

Elizabeth admits she has not. Not yet.

The Taylor-Grady House is available as a rental venue for weddings and special occasions, and is open for tours on weekdays.

The Taylor-Grady House
References

Davis, Melissa. "Ghosts Among the Kudzu." *DigitalCommons@Kennesaw State University*. Kennesaw State University. Web.

Head, Matthew. "Ghosts of Athens, GA (Long but Good!)." *Google Groups*. Newsgroup post. 3 May 1999.

"History." The Junior league of Athens. Web. 09 Sept. 2016. <http://www.juniorleagueofathens.org/history>.

Matthews, Dan. "Ghost Tour Showcases Clarke and Oconee Haunts." Online Athens. *Athens Banner-Herald*. Web. 09 Sept. 2016.

"Namesakes." The Taylor Grady House. Web. 09 Sept. 2016. <http://www.taylorgradyhouse.com/namesakes/>.

"Through the Years." The Taylor Grady House. Web. 09 Sept. 2016. <http://www.taylorgradyhouse.com/other-owners/>.

Wikipedia contributors. "Henry W. Grady House." *Wikipedia, The Free Encyclopedia*. 2 Jul. 2016. Web. 9 Sep. 2016.

Author interview with Taylor-Grady House employee Elizabeth Elliott

MEMORIAL PARK

Nestled in the Five Points neighborhood, Memorial Park is part of the Athens-Clarke County Leisure Services Department and is one of the most popular locations in Athens for families to visit. The 72-acre park has a storied past, beginning as the site of a medical facility.

Memorial Park was originally built in 1925 as a tuberculosis sanatorium called Fairhaven Hospital. Women's organizations, including the Athens Women's Club and Athens Junior Assembly, were actively involved in public health issues and played a major role in the funding of the facility.

Fairhaven Hospital was constructed in the Spanish Colonial Revival architectural style. This style, which was the height of fashion from 1915 to 1940 and common for landmark buildings in Florida and the Southwest, was unusual in the Athens area.

During the 1920s, the facility was a major factor in the fight waged against epidemic levels of tuberculosis. In May of 1926, the *Athens Banner-Herald* reported that the county had gained national recognition for its tuberculosis efforts.

According to James Reap's book, *A Pictorial History*, in Fairhaven Hospital "thirty beds were equally distributed between black and white patients." This would have been cutting edge for a hospital at that time.

Later, during the 1930s, Fairhaven patients were transferred to a larger state facility. In the late 1940s, the hospital and grounds were converted by the city for use as a park.

In 1946, Memorial Park was dedicated and opened to the public. It included a pond and day camp. This facility played a major role in providing the Athens community with recreation activities. In 1958, the Teen Canteen was dedicated and remained a favorite social spot for area teens for decades.

More recent additions to the park include a swimming pool, the Birchmore Trail, two basketball courts, and a playground. Additionally, the park is the home of Athens Creative Theatre. In 2004, the park office buildings were renovated.

The park also boasts Bear Hollow Zoo and an animal health care facility. The zoo is home to Georgia's native wildlife in natural habitat exhibits that are used to teach about wildlife and the environment. Resident animals include bears, bobcats, deer, otters, owls, a bald eagle, and more than 120 species of wild animals. The exhibit hall, which features amphibians and reptiles, is open to the public and features projects for younger visitors and live animals to see and touch.

For some park employees, the critters are not the most fearsome residents at the location. When I spoke with John McKinney, Facility Supervisor at Memorial Park, I asked him about paranormal events in the building. He began by saying that some events that seem strange on the surface can usually be explained away when considered rationally. This included random instances of squeaking floors and toilets that regularly flush with no one around. Around the year 2010, the building hosted a haunted house for a Halloween celebration, but resident spooks chose not to cooperate or contribute to the festivities on that night.

Around the same time period, a park employee had a more eventful experience in the building, as McKinney described to me:

"Memorial Park stays open until sunset," he said. "One night, as evening fell, one of the park assistants named Ben was the last one left in the building. He was in the office located in this wing, then went down to the Recreation Hall in the opposite wing.

"In the Rec Hall, he closed all the blinds, turned off all the lights, and set the alarm. Then, he came back over here to the office. He happened to look through the window that looks out towards the Rec Hall. Across the way in the recreation hall windows, he saw the blinds move, as if someone used their fingers to open them to look through the window, right at him.

"Even though he knew nobody was down there, Ben went back to the other wing, back down to the recreation hall to double check if someone was in there when they weren't supposed to be. When he got to the Rec Hall, all of the blinds were wide open even though he had closed him himself only moments before.

"This unnerved Ben, so he returned to the office and began locking up to leave. Just as he was about to reach the front door and make his exit, a child's voice came from thin air in the hallway: 'Goodnight, Ben.'

"Ben dashed through the front door, locked it tight and didn't look back as he hurried away."

Another employee was working at the park late one night. He was the last one to leave and locking up for the night. As he stood at the end of the hallway between the office wing and the Recreation Hall wing, he saw the outline of a figure at the end of the hall near the doors to the Rec Hall. Rather than investigate, he chose to shut the door, turn off the lights and leave.

Park employees are not the only ones who have suffered through frightening encounters.

One summer, the park had contracted with a cleaning service. The cleaning crew would come in to clean in the building after hours. One woman on the cleaning crew was so disturbed by what she witnessed, she eventually told the park managers that she did not want to clean in the building after dark.

"During that time, summer camp activities ran until 6 p.m.," McKinney explained. "Then, when all the campers were gone home, she would come in and clean. But, when she was in the building in the evenings all alone, she would hear things and feel a creepy sensation that she was, in fact, not alone.

"After refusing to stay in the building alone at night, she was allowed to come in early in the morning instead to complete her cleaning duties."

This was not a foolproof plan, however. One morning as she cleaned, she once again sensed that she was not alone in the room. It occurred to her to snap a photo to try to obtain evidence of the something that was hanging around.

When she examined the picture, she was shocked to find that the picture showed a shadowy outline of the lower part of a person's body. Where no one had been in the room with her, "a pair of legs was standing silhouetted against the wall," McKinney described. "She sent me the picture."

Instead of making her more afraid of the building, the experience seemed to have the opposite effect. After that incident, the woman said she became friends with the ghost. She even resumed coming in to clean at night and did not have any problems doing so. She claimed that the ghost didn't bother her anymore.

Marla Whittington, Administrative Secretary at the park, recalls earlier days when the park's spooky history was part of local lore.

"I went to high school at Clarke Central High School. When we were teenagers, we would dare each other to sleep here in the park in the dark after the gates had been locked. Kids would come down to the lake in the dark and hang out on the benches.

"I wasn't brave enough to do it. In the winter, it gets pretty darn dark. There are no lights except for a bit from the houses behind the park. I'd only get about halfway down the hill.

"But, I have felt weird in this building," she admitted.

An event she cannot explain involves a squeaky stall door in the bathroom. She described how she would be sitting in her office in the middle of the day and hear the stall door down the hall slowly squeak open with no one around. She wryly wondered, "Is that a person or a Moaning Myrtle?"

"My son used to come here for summer camp a long time ago," Marla continued. "Once, he was walking in the hallway and suddenly felt like someone was puffing air in his face, even though no one was there in the hall with him." The air puffing had occurred in the hallway near the bathroom. He told his mother he refused to use that bathroom in the hallway ever again. Afterward, whenever he needed to go, he chose to go outside and all the way around to the bathroom at the pool rather than risk another encounter with the hallway air puffer.

"We thought he just didn't want to come back to summer camp, like the time when he got pulled into the lake by a goose and cried for three days." Later, Marla found out that the building had previously been a tuberculosis hospital. "That ghost cold have been struggling for breath or coughing," she conceded. "That might have been what he felt."

Memorial Park is located at 293 Gran Ellen Drive and is open daily.

Undated photo of Memorial Park (above)
Photo courtesy of Memorial Park

Memorial Park prior to the 2004 remodel (above)
Photo courtesy of Memorial Park

Memorial Park
References

"Bear Hollow Zoo." Athens-Clarke County, GA. Web. 09 Sept. 2016. <http://www.athensclarkecounty.com/Facilities/Facility/Details/1>.

"Bear Hollow Zoo | Athens, Georgia." Official Website of the Georgia Department of Economic Development. 09 Sept. 2016. Web. 09 Sept. 2016. <http://www.exploregeorgia.org/listing/371-bear-hollow-zoo>.

"Memorial Park." Athens-Clarke County, GA. Web. 09 Sept. 2016. <http://athensclarkecounty.com/Facilities/Facility/Details/12>.

Reap, James K. Athens, a Pictorial History. Virginia Beach, VA: Donning, 1985. Print.

"Grand Reopening of the Memorial Park Operations Center" Memorial Park event program. 2004.

Author interview with Memorial Park Facility Supervisor John McKinney

Memorial Park history booklet shared by John McKinney.

Author interview with Memorial Park Administrative Secretary Marla Whittington

OLD ATHENS CEMETERY

The Old Athens Cemetery, also known as the Jackson Street Cemetery, was the original burial ground for the city of Athens. The land where it is located was part of the original tract of land purchased in 1801 by Governor John Milledge to create the University of Georgia.

The six-acre cemetery on the University's North Campus was founded in the early 1800s and primarily used between 1810 and 1856. According to the historical marker on site, all Athenians were allowed to bury their dead there free of charge. It was also a burial ground for University students who died at school and could not be returned home.

Those buried there include merchants, tailors, ministers, children of UGA faculty members, two soldiers from the Revolutionary War, and two UGA presidents: Robert Finley and Moses Waddel. Some of the grave markers are inscribed local fieldstones and others are made from imported marble.

In 1856, when the cemetery was overcrowded with more than 800 graves, additional burials were prohibited. The last known burial occurred in 1898.

As late as 1906, the cemetery remained as six acres, intact. Today, the cemetery occupies only 2.5 acres. As the University and town of Athens grew all around it, cemetery land was usurped for other purposes.

In 1890, Chancellor Walter B. Hill had the idea to overtake the cemetery property for new land to relieve the overcrowded University. He proposed to move all of the graves to the new Oconee Hill Cemetery in order to erect new University buildings on the land. Due to vigorous opposition, the idea did not succeed. His death in December of 1905 ended this campaign.

Again in 1920, the University proposed to take over the cemetery land and this time succeeded. Several acres were taken from the south end of the cemetery for the construction of Baldwin Hall and its adjoining parking lot. In 1960, before construction of the Visual Arts Building, the University had the cemetery land in its sights. Fortunately, the Athens Historical Society put a stop to it. Finally, in 1980, the University again proposed to move all gravesites to the Oconee Hill Cemetery in order to build a parking deck. This was successfully halted by a group that later became the Old Athens Cemetery Foundation.

Ironically, the cemetery land was deeded back to the University in 2004. They seem to have no further designs to pave or otherwise destroy the cemetery since, in 2006, the University of Georgia Grounds Department began a preservation program for it.

Supposedly, at the time the acreage was repurposed, the bodies and headstones were both relocated, but more often than not, only the headstones were actually moved. One can only imagine the large population of gravesites now located beneath the roads, buildings and walkways surrounding the cemetery now. In fact, on occasion, one doesn't need to imagine at all. When the University does construction anywhere in the vicinity, they are likely to get more than they bargained for.

In 2015, a construction crew renovating Baldwin Hall, located on Jackson Street near the cemetery, had the misfortune to unearth a human skull. All work at the site was brought to a halt as the University worked with state agencies to investigate the area. Ultimately, twenty-seven graves were located. All of them were disinterred and relocated.

Some people familiar with the history of the cemetery feel certain that the interred residents must be displeased with the way the grounds have been treated as less-than-sacred, particularly the ones that have been built or paved over. This leads ghost hunters to seek out the location for investigation. The Georgia Haunt Hunters investigated in 1998 and recorded unusual temperature fluctuations.

One Georgia blogger with an interest in the paranormal visited the cemetery grounds years ago. She reported that when she tried to take photos of the grave markers, the cameras repeatedly malfunctioned. The digital images recorded showed none of the headstones or grounds. The pictures were almost all white, as if a bright light had blocked the image. She also saw light anomalies using the camera display screen.

"As I am aiming the camera, I look in the picture screen and see a light jumping at the base of a tomb. I call my husband over to see if he sees it too. Neither one of us can see it without the camera, and it doesn't show up in the pictures, but both of us can see it through the display screen... it's deliciously spooky."

University of Georgia employee Carol Bishop also participated in an investigation at the cemetery. "I was in a ghost hunting group in the 90s," Bishop told me. "We went to the Jackson Street Cemetery. We were detecting strong drops in temperatures. We got pictures of big orbs floating around."

Bishop also recalls when the University unearthed bodies during construction near the cemetery. "They were remodeling on Baldwin Street and they dug up a bunch of corpses over there. When they were creating the sidewalk between the cemetery and the old art building, they dug up a perfectly preserved corpse. Thirty years ago, they found some on the north side. They're all over the place."

Author Terry Morgan published a *Red and Black* newspaper article that described the folklore of the Old Athens Cemetery:

> One foggy Halloween night, Wee Willie headed for home on the railroad tracks toward the Oconee River. But he didn't make it home that night.
>
> "A train did not see him on the tracks and hit him. It destroyed his head," says Jack Thomas, a columnist for a local newspaper who heard about Wee Willie from his grandfather. "The police came and took his body, but not his head."
>
> Now, folks say, poor Willie's head propels itself down the railroad tracks, screaming and searching for its body. Athens has its share of ghosts and spirits, and on Halloween night one can see them haunting the cemetery or house that serves as their final resting place.
>
> Willie wandered into Athens in the 1930s and no one knew where he came from. His short stature earned him his nickname.
>
> Thomas' grandfather once owned a saloon on College Avenue, where Wee Willie did chores for him. "Wee Willie supposedly slept in a hollow log somewhere on the Oconee River," Thomas says. "He always toted a croaker sack, which you know as a burlap sack."
>
> No one knows why he came to Athens, but he evidently didn't bother anyone. People often hired him to do odd jobs around their houses.
>
> After he was killed, two little boys found Willie's sack on the bank of the Oconee River," Thomas says: "They picked it up, and before they could look in it, a scream came from it."

Naturally, the boys ran. When they returned later, the sack was gone, and no one ever saw it again. Thomas says no one knew what Willie carried in his sack, because he never opened it in front of anybody. "There were houses in that area at that time. These were more like shacks where the poor people lived — they've all been torn down since then. But after Willie was killed, many people moved out because they were scared," says one University faculty member who wishes to remain anonymous.

Willie's headless body was buried in an unmarked grave in the cemetery on Jackson Street between the Visual Arts Building and Baldwin Hall.

This cemetery, known as the Old Athens Cemetery, was the first graveyard in Athens. According to Patricia Cooper of the Old Athens Cemetery Foundation, the earliest known burial there is believed to have been that of a Mrs. Lane in 1794. Legend states Mrs. Lane was fleeing an Indian attack in Oglethorpe County, and she died from the cold in the Athens area. Her body was buried, but no tombstone was erected to indicate its location.

Another story connected with the cemetery concerns Chancellor Walter B. Hill (1899-1905). Hill wanted to rid the campus of the cemetery and, according to Cooper, was "punished" for doing so." He (Hill) had the idea of using the land for some other purpose and moving the graves to Oconee Hills (Cemetery)," Cooper says. "He was walking one day through the graveyard, thinking about his plans," she says. "It was winter, and he walked through the cold, wet grass." Soon after, Hill caught a chill that developed into pneumonia, and he died in 1905. Perhaps the spirits of the bodies he planned to move sought revenge, Cooper says.

One wonders if Chancellor Hill would choose to haunt the cemetery that brought him so much grief, even though his place of burial is the Oconee Hill Cemetery.

When visitors first enter the gates of the cemetery, one of the first headstones they see belongs to Dicy Ann Roberts. Dicy Ann was born in 1839 and shows on the Clarke County Georgia census for the year 1850. Her headstone indicates she died on July 3rd, 1852 at age thirteen.

No one is sure what caused her tragic death at such a young age, but some who have reported seeing the image of a young girl running around in the cemetery are inclined to believe it is her.

Though the census places her in Athens, her headstone is engraved with, "daughter of Thomas Roberts of Cleaveland, NC." This leads one local researcher to theorize that Dicy Ann is looking for her family. "Perhaps she was buried by someone with money since she does have a headstone," she suggested. "Maybe she was visiting here, got sick, and had no other family."

According to Bishop, numerous people have reporting seeing the shadowy figure of a young girl dressed in a long dress wandering around the cemetery. A ghost-hunting group believes that they have captured her image on film.

Bishop also relates the following strange tale:

> The February 2, 1897 issue of *The Athens Banner-Herald* recounts a strange event that took place the evening before. The residents of Mrs. Gilleland's boarding house on Jackson Street were awakened by a terrible noise coming from the adjacent cemetery. They notified the police who found a 40-year-old man in the center of the graveyard kneeling in front of one the graves. He was moaning and uncontrollably crying. As the police arrived they noted that he also started praying in a very wild and incoherent manner.
>
> The police took him in and upon examination; they said he hadn't been drinking at all. The only thing the man was able to tell them was that he was a stonecutter from Atlanta and he had

no idea how he had gotten to Athens or why he was in the middle of the cemetery in the dead of night.

The Old Athens Cemetery underwent cleaning and repairs during restoration from 2007 to 2009 and was added to the National Register of Historic Places in October of 2009. By clearing vegetation overgrowth and repairing monuments, restoration efforts by the University of Georgia Grounds Department to combat vandalism and weathering are ongoing.

IMPORTANT NOTE: THE GROUNDS OF THE OLD ATHENS CEMETERY ARE CURRENTLY GATED AND ACCESS IS RESTRICTED. IF YOU VISIT THE OLD ATHENS CEMETERY, GAIN PERMISSION FOR APPROPRIATE ACCESS TO THE PROPERTY, HAVE RESPECT FOR THE GROUNDS AND BURIAL SITES, AND ABIDE BY ALL RESTRICTIONS TO MAINTAIN THIS IMPORTANT PART OF ATHENS HISTORY.

The Old Athens Cemetery (Jackson Street Cemetery)

Dicy Ann's headstone

Walkway over the dead beside the Old Athens Cemetery

Old Athens Cemetery
References

Bishop, Carol. "Haunted North Campus Walking Tour Script". Athens-Clarke Heritage Foundation tour on July 20, 2010.

Head, Matthew. "Ghosts of Athens, GA (Long but Good!)." *Google Groups.* Newsgroup post. 3 May 1999.

Davis, Melissa. "Ghosts Among the Kudzu." DigitalCommons@Kennesaw State University. Kennesaw State University. Web.

Morgan, Terry. "Athens has its share of ghastly ghouls and Halloween horrors." *The Red and Black.* (Undated clipping from the Georgia Ghosts folder in the Hargrett Library collection.)

"Jackson Street Cemetery - Old Athens Cemetery." Athens Life Unleashed. Visitathensga.com. Web. 09 Sept. 2016.

"Old Athens Cemetery." Georgia On My Mind. Exploregeorgia.org. Web.

Wikipedia contributors. "Jackson Street Cemetery." Wikipedia, The Free Encyclopedia. Wikipedia, The Free Encyclopedia, 29 Jun. 2016. Web. 9 Sep. 2016.

LexCBlount. "Haunted Places of Georgia- Our Scavenger Hunt of Creepy Haunts." Spooky Seeking, Legend Hunting, & Hidden Places:. Blogspot.com, 09 Sept. 2016. Web. 09 Sept. 2016.

Caldwell, Tami. "1850 Federal Census Clarke County, Georgia." Usgwarchives.net. The USGenWeb Census Project, 2000. Web. 09 Sept. 2016.

Author interview with a local researcher for the Athens-Clarke Heritage Foundation

Author interview with Carol Bishop, Librarian for the University Archives at the University of Georgia

Author interview with Gilbert Head, Archival Associate for the University Archives at the University of Georgia

OCONEE HILL CEMETERY

While the Sanford Stadium is commonly filled to capacity with raucous football fans, just down the hill behind the stadium, a different, silent crowd is gathered, and all of them are underground.

Historic Oconee Hill Cemetery is located at 297 Cemetery Street. Its gates are literally in the shadow of Sanford Stadium.

Originally, deceased Athenians were interred on available land on the University of Georgia North Campus and in the Old Athens Cemetery. But, after a time, overcrowded campus burials occurred disturbingly close to housing and offices for the University President and professors. When new burials were prohibited in the old cemetery, this spurred University trustees to urge the mayor to create a new public cemetery.

In 1855, the city of Athens spent $1,000 to purchase seventeen acres of land beside the Oconee River for the new cemetery. In 1856, Oconee Hill Cemetery was formally established. A plan for the cemetery's design was adopted, a self-perpetuating governing board was installed, and the first lots were auctioned.

James Camak, a prominent member of the University of Georgia's faculty designed the Oconee Hill Cemetery based on his familiarity with the Victorian rural cemetery movement, in fashion at the time. This movement incorporated trees, grassy and rolling terrain, flowing water, meandering drives, and scenic vistas. The result was commonly more reminiscent of an arboretum or botanical garden than a cemetery. This design makes the cemetery a surprisingly pleasant place to visit, at least in the daytime.

Besides the landscape design, Oconee Hill Cemetery also has decorative funerary markers, unique cast-iron fencing, and a Sexton's House. In 1892, the Sexton's House was purchased from the adjoining Athens Manufacturing Company and served as the sexton's residence for the next 90 years. Diverse architectural styles appear in the mausoleums—obelisks, headstones, and other markers, including Greek Revival, Gothic Revival, High Victorian Gothic, and Egyptian Revival.

If you stroll the grounds, you may notice that some grave markers predate the cemetery opening in 1856. This is because some graves were relocated there over time from the Old Athens Cemetery and other family plots and church cemeteries.

The same year Oconee Hill Cemetery was established, almost all the available lots were sold, so in 1898, the trustees enlarged the cemetery by 82 acres. To reach the new section, the city built a 150-foot bridge across the Oconee River in 1899. The iron-and-steel Pratt bridge is among the few through-truss bridges in the state.

Unusual for the early 19th century, the Oconee Hill Cemetery has always been accepting of all races. It includes a segregated section for African-American burials, although some of those graves are poorly marked. Distinctive designs also adorn Jewish burial markers.

Also interred at the cemetery are four Confederate generals and veterans of all American wars, including the American Revolution. Many political figures found their final resting place here, including former U.S. Secretary of State Dean Rusk, two Georgia governors—Wilson Lumpkin and Howell Cobb, and the first chief justice of the Georgia Supreme Court, Joseph Henry Lumpkin. Crawford Long, discoverer of anesthesia, and Georgia's first aviator, Ben Epps, are buried here as well.

Now listed on the National Register of Historic Places, the Oconee Hill Cemetery is currently comprised of one hundred acres. The Sexton's House was restored in 2007 by the Friends of Oconee Hill Cemetery.

The haunted reputation of the Oconee Hill Cemetery may stem from incidents early on in its history. For example, it is rumored that when bodies previously interred at the Old Athens Cemetery were relocated to the new cemetery, the headstones were moved but the bodies were left behind. Perhaps agitated spirits want visitors to know that the graves are not what they seem.

Gilbert Head, Archival Associate for the University Archives says of the cemetery: "There has been some grave-disturbing going on there. Supposedly, during the course of one excavation, a coffin slid out, the lid popped open, and the guy sat up dressed in the manner someone would have been in the 1870s. But, there were no authorized burials from that time period.

"We do know there are graves there that do not have markers because ground-penetrating radar has found them. There are a substantial number of graves that don't have markers. It is not known if this was unauthorized and done in secret or if they are pauper's graves or if a marker that was previously there has been taken away."

Head laments that damage to the cemetery continued into recent history with vandalism being committed by undergrads and football tailgaters.

In 1902, The Athens Weekly Banner published a story about adventure-seekers who claimed a run-in with a ghost in the cemetery. Residents living near the Oconee Hill Cemetery reported seeing the figure of a ghostly woman dressed in an old-timey outfit. A few brave students wanted to investigate. They got permission from the sexton to spend the night in the cemetery and set up camp in the area where the spooky woman had been spotted.

Based on the newspaper account, the men saw the figure of a woman slowly rise up from a grave. At first, she appeared airy and phantom-like but slowly morphed into the shape of a goat. As soon as the figure was well-defined, the goat leapt to the bank of the river, plunged headlong into the current, and disappeared.

A relevant side-note to this tale is that the original football mascot at the University was a goat, as evidenced by numerous creepy illustrations of goats in UGA's yearbook, Pandora. Though none can now say what true events transpired that night, we can be sure that newspaper readers and football fans alike were entertained by the story.

Other folklore suggests that a mysterious light shaped like a lantern can be seen by sitting on a bench across from a certain tombstone. Another story about the cemetery bridge suggests that a troll lives beneath it. If you are on the bridge, you can turn your back and throw a penny over your shoulder off the side, but the penny won't fall and make any sound because the greedy troll snatches it up.

One pervasive tale is told regarding the cemetery bridge that crosses the river, connecting the old part of the cemetery with the new. In years past, the bridge through the cemetery was used by students (including myself) as a shortcut to get to classes on campus from their apartments on the opposite side of the river. It is true that few braved that path after the sun went down.

This path has been inaccessible for students to use in recent years. But, back when they did, some would challenge their friends to prove their bravery by visiting the cemetery bridge on the night of a full moon. Rumor held that if you patiently waited below the bridge, you would witness an event that would turn your blood cold.

This rumor was based on a decades-old tale about a local farmer who had a big night in town and over-indulged in drink. Rushing home with horse and buggy, he whipped the horse to faster and faster speeds. The wagon was crossing the bridge at top speed when the farmer lost control and veered over the side. Horse, buggy, and driver all careened off the bridge and down into the rushing waters below. The farmer and the horse were both killed.

Afterward, locals insisted that at midnight on the night of a full moon, if you waited at the bottom of the bridge you would eventually hear horse hooves approaching in the distance. Closer and closer, the sounds approached in the night, until the clopping of horse hooves and clattering of wagon wheels crossed directly overhead on the bridge. This was the sound of the farmer attempting to complete his unfinished journey.

Supposedly, the farmer's body is buried in the cemetery very near the bridge where he met his demise.

IMPORTANT NOTE: ALTHOUGH STORIES ABOUT THE CEMETERY'S PAST INCLUDE TALES OF MIDNIGHT VISITS AND OTHER ADVENTURES, THE CEMETERY NOW HAS A STRICT POLICY REGARDING APPROPRIATE ACCESS TO THE PROPERTY. IF YOU VISIT OCONEE HILL CEMETERY, PLEASE DO ENJOY THE BEAUTY AND HISTORY THAT ABOUNDS AND HAVE RESPECT FOR THE GROUNDS, BURIAL SITES AND VISITING FAMILY MEMBERS. ABIDE BY ALL RESTRICTIONS TO MAINTAIN THIS IMPORTANT PART OF ATHENS HISTORY.

Statuary at Oconee Hill Cemetery

Statuary at Oconee Hill Cemetery

Oconee Hill Cemetery
References

Bishop, Carol. "Haunted North Campus Walking Tour Script". Athens-Clarke Heritage Foundation tour on July 20, 2010.

Davis, Melissa. "Ghosts Among the Kudzu." *DigitalCommons@Kennesaw State University*. Kennesaw State University. Web.

Head, Matthew. "Ghosts of Athens, GA (Long but Good!)." *Google Groups*. Newsgroup post. 3 May 1999.

"Oconee Hill Cemetery." Oconee Hill Cemetery. Web. 09 Sept. 2016. <http://www.oconeehillcemetery.com/>.

Author interview with Carol Bishop, Librarian for the University Archives at the University of Georgia

Author interview with Steven Brown, University Archivist Emeritus

ARNOCROFT

In 1903, Oliver Hazzard Arnold, Jr. acquired a ten-acre property surrounded by Milledge Avenue, Rutherford Street, and Lumpkin Street. Oliver Arnold was married to Aurie Baynes Arnold, and they had three daughters: Jennie, Elizabeth and Eugenia. From 1924 to 1925, Arnold was the mayor of Athens, Georgia.

Arnold relocated his family to the spacious property after building a white frame Victorian with a wraparound porch at 925 South Milledge Avenue. The house was called Arnocroft: "Arno," taken from the family name, and "Croft," which is a plot of arable land attached to a house.

The home was remodeled in 1933 to have a stylish Colonial Revival appearance. The clapboard exterior gave way to a red brick facade. The front door was of Federal style.

"They were not only wealthy; they were wealthy through the Depression. Mr. Arnold used that project to put people to work," said Sandi Turner, who grew up down the street from the Arnocroft house. "The look that you see now when you drive down Milledge is a result of that project that he undertook.

"There are a lot of interesting elements of the house," she continued, "One of which is there was a back sleeping-porch that was built entirely of Piedmont-area wood. All the furnishings and cabinetry was the work of Piedmont-area artisans. That was also added as part of the Depression-era renovation."

In 1935, when the population of Athens, Georgia was less than 20,000, Eugenia Arnold was the founding president of the Junior League of Athens, known then as the Athens Junior Assembly. The Junior Assembly created a way for young women to spend their leisure hours to meet welfare needs of the town and was a source of charity and maternity and baby care.

Eleven short years after remodeling his home, Oliver Arnold passed away in 1944 at age 77. Over time, the original ten acres was subdivided and sold off, but Arnocroft remained in the family. Widow Aurie Arnold and daughter Eugenia began to spend a great deal of time traveling.

"The family traveled like crazy. Mrs. Arnold and her daughter Eugenia traveled like crazy and they shopped like crazy," said Turner. "When you entered the house, on the left-hand side of the front door, there was a ballroom. In that ballroom, there was a magnificent rug that came from some down-on-their-luck Russian aristocrat. The whole house was full of treasures like that from their travels."

Eugenia was in her thirties when she settled down and got married to John J. Blount. Tragically, after waiting many years to find love, her husband died only a year later.

According to Turner, "Eugenia spent the next 20-plus years traveling with her mother and then traveling on her own after her mother died." During Aurie and Eugenia's travels throughout Europe and America, they brought home many furnishings and objects d'art from their excursions.

According to Turner, Eugenia did eventually find love again. "Somewhere in her later years, during the early 1970s, she met a man from Philadelphia, Mr. Ted Friend," said Turner. "What attracted them to each other was a love of travel. They got married and traveled a lot together."

Because Mr. Friend was from Philadelphia, the couple would spend half the year there. At the Arnocroft house, they would cover the furniture and close the shutters while they were gone for six months. Then, they would come home and open the shutters and dust everything off to live in Athens for the rest of the year.

"The story goes that when she returned to Athens to stay, she would raise a flag that had a martini glass on it. That flag meant that she was open for business, to come over for drinks. She entertained lavishly when she was in town," Turner says. "I grew up on Woodlawn Avenue, just a few streets down on Milledge and I graduated from Clarke Central High School in 1987. I don't remember the martini flag, but I definitely remember the shuttered windows, because, all through my high school years, the rumor was that that house was haunted. The shuttered windows definitely gave it that vibe."

Eugenia Arnold Blount Friend died in 1994. Her many years associated with the Junior League influenced her to bequeath to the group Arnocroft and two acres, along with $400,000 for upkeep. The house included the entire collection of lavish furnishings and decorative arts collected by Aurie, Eugenia and the extended Arnold family over their lifetimes. Many of these pieces were unique examples of design and craftsmanship and were recognized in a special exhibit at the Georgia Museum of Art in 1998.

Eugenia specifically stipulated that the house could not be sold and was to be kept as it was at the time of her death. She further specified that the house continue to be known as Arnocroft, and it was to be used to "...further the interest and welfare of the people of the community of Athens."

However, in late 2006, the Junior League asked an Athens-Clarke County Superior Court judge for permission to give up the house, saying it had become too expensive to keep up. The property tax bill had grown to $20,000 per year, according to court records. The Junior League's request was granted in December 2006 and the property reverted to Eugenia's heirs, who sold the property to a fraternity in May 2008. The Athens Chi Phi chapter paid $1.7 million for the property.

Sandi Turner's knowledge of Arnocroft eventually encompassed more than just anxious stares at the cold shuttered house on walks to and from school. "When I was president of the Athens Junior League, I was absolutely delighted to get the chance to explore Arnocroft after hearing the stories for so long that it was haunted," she told me.

"I was making arrangements for the board council retreat the year that I was taking over as president because I wanted us to utilize the house. The Junior League acquired the house in 1996 and I was president in 2000. For those four years between, nobody had really done anything there except one party. The membership was really disconnected from it. As kind of a symbolic gesture, I did my board council retreat there to try to get people interested and try to start to use the house.

"The problem with this idea was that there was no air conditioning. The unit had literally been taken out of the house. We were doing work in the house and spent a good bit of money shoring up pilings and doing things to protect the structural integrity. In the course of that work, air systems were taken completely away.

"And there was not a lot of power. Some places the power worked and some places it didn't. The board council retreat was typically in the summer, in August. So, August comes around and we're going to have this retreat and it's hot as all get out. I went and got electrical cords and found electrical sockets that worked and plugged fans in to try to give us some relief.

"While in Arnocroft during the retreat, at some point I stepped on top of an air conditioning grate, and there was air conditioning coming out of it. This was despite there being no air conditioning unit, literally no unit in the house. That was like, whoa, this is weird! At the time, we thought that happened because Eugenia wanted us there and she brought us air conditioning. She was happy that I was using the house after it sat silent for all those years.

"There's absolutely, literally no logical explanation for that air conditioner working. There were a lot of people in the house. It wasn't like I was over there on my own and my imagination got the best of me. It didn't just happen for a little while. This went on for the whole time we were there. It was hot as the blazes. We had the fans going all over the place. But this was full-on cool air. Like air conditioner air.

"I've tried for years to think of a logical explanation for that and never came up with anything," Turner told me.

Similar tricks were played with the ancient lighting in the house. "A light fixture had been disconnected but when you drop by the house, the light would be on," Turner recalled. When she told the story to other members, they responded, "Oh, yeah. That happens all the time."

On another occasion, it seemed Eugenia did not care for how she was being handled by a Junior League member. Some members were in the home working to refurbish it for use when one member was injured.

"We were moving stuff around in the house and there was a giant portrait of Eugenia in the sitting room," said Turner. "For some reason, the Chair of the Arnocroft house wanted to take the portrait down off the wall. In doing so, she cut her finger. As a result, there was a streak of blood from her finger that ran down the wall. She put the portrait down and she went to clean her finger.

"When we went back into the sitting room later the next day, that streak of blood was still bright red, like she had just cut her finger a moment ago. It had not turned black like blood should have. We all thought that was really creepy."

Turner told me that most all League members who worked in the house had a strange story to relate. They often would go in the house to work on a task and leave things a certain way when they left. When they came back later, knowing no one else had been there, they would find the items they left had been moved around.

As another example, the home included a large doll collection. "There was a big doll collection with some really creepy dolls," Turner confided. "You know those dolls they used to do at the turn of the century that were like a kid's actual face? There was one doll that we all found extremely disturbing. It looked just like the pictures we had of Mr. Arnold." According to Turner, the dolls managed to move around from one place to another in the house with no ready explanation.

One can image that Eugenia is not pleased that her treasured home has become a fraternity dwelling. If so, she is likely making her displeasure known to the current residents.

Arnocroft References

Aued, Blake. "Frat to Rework Arnocroft Plan." *Onlineathens.com*. *Athens Banner-Herald*, 3 Sept. 2010. Web.

"Eugenia Arnold." *Ancestry.com*. Ancestry.com. Web. 09 Sept. 2016. <http://www.ancestry.com/genealogy/records/eugenia-arnold_115307532>.

"History." *Junior League of Athens*. Junior League of Athens. Web. 09 Sept. 2016. <http://www.juniorleagueofathens.org/history>.

"Milledge House Has Fraternity's Eye." *Onlineathens.com*. *Athens Banner-Herald*, 3 July 2008. Web.

Moon, Allison. "Assessing the Feasibility of Using Arnocroft as an Historic House Museum." *Getd.libs.uga.edu*. Getd.libs.uga.edu, 1999. Web. <https://getd.libs.uga.edu/pdfs/moon_allison_a_200405_mhp.pdf>.

"Past Presidents." *Junior League of Athens*. Junior League of Athens. Web. 09 Sept. 2016. <http://www.juniorleagueofathens.org/past-presidents>.

The Athens-Clarke Heritage Foundation Walking Tour. http://www.athenswelcomecenter.com/images/milledge_ave_walking_tour.pdf

Author interview with Junior league member Sandi Turner

SUNTRUST BANK

The SunTrust Bank at 1022 Prince Avenue does not look like your typical bank. The stately, historic home is also known as the Stephen Upson House and has a long history with the city of Athens.

Prince Avenue, where the bank is located, is named for Oliver Prince, a Macon, Georgia lawyer and railroad developer whose farm was in the vicinity. In 1847, Dr. Marcus A. Franklin purchased seven acres from the estate of Oliver Prince to build a plantation home.

At that time, the population of Athens was approximately 3,000 people, making it the fifth-largest city in the state, larger than Atlanta or Milledgeville. The University of Georgia had 133 students enrolled and Watkinsville was the county seat.

The home built by Dr. Franklin was a 4,400-square-foot Greek Revival structure with ceilings on the first floor more than twelve feet high. Dr. Franklin sold the home in 1848 to Gazaway Lamar, and in 1853, it sold to James Long, father of Dr. Crawford W. Long. The home changed hands twice more until, in 1885, the home was purchased by the family of Stephen C. Upson.

The Upson family had a storied career in law. Stephen Upson descended from Joseph Henry Lumpkin, the first chief justice of the Supreme Court of Georgia and founder of the Lumpkin Law School at the University of Georgia. Stephen Upson was a Yale trustee and pre-Civil War lawyer and Upson County, Georgia was named for him. Stephen C. Upson himself practiced and taught law. Young Stephen Lumpkin Upson, who grew up in the Upson House, went on to be a successful lawyer as well, and lived until 2005 at age 97.

After purchasing the home, Stephen Upson added a new kitchen to the rear of the original structure and installed herringbone oak parquet floors with inlaid borders of mahogany and rosewood. The doorknobs and keyhole covers were pure silver. Elegant architecture and furnishings made the home a standout in nineteenth-century Athens.

Over the years, the parlor was decorated with Vieux Paris vases and original Chippendale chairs. A portrait of Stephen Upson was hung along with other portraits from the 1700s.

Louise Upson Foss was sister to Stephen Lumpkin Upson and the granddaughter of Mrs. Edwin King Lumpkin, the founder of the first garden club in America. Foss was the fourth generation to stay in the Upson House and was pleased when, in 1973, the home was added to the National Register of Historic Places.

In 1974, the Upson House was in need of substantial repairs and was sold to the First National Bank of Athens with a stipulation to preserve the historic home. The house was adapted for use as a banking office and more than 1,500 square feet of office space was added at the rear of the property. Care was taken to preserve many large magnolias and other rare trees.

SunTrust Bank

Five months of restorations by architectural specialists from Atlanta included installing a new roof, restoring stucco, replacing triple-sash windows, restoring plaster, and installation of ceiling medallions. Completed in 1979, the result duplicated the home's appearance from the time Stephen Upson occupied it.

Derrick Allen is currently a Teller Coordinator for the SunTrust bank in the Stephen Upson House. He has worked for the bank for four years and is not surprised when someone tells him that they have experienced something unusual there.

"I've also had people say that they've seen shadowy figures in the upstairs windows when driving by the branch on the weekends," he told me. "This branch is closed on weekends."

Allen has also had clients tell him that the location of the bank teller station was originally a bedroom where, reportedly, one of the residents died.

Not all of Allen's spooky knowledge relies on hearsay. He has had an experience of his own. "About two years ago, I was clearing the branch one morning before business hours," he shared. "I was in the branch by myself. I walked through a doorway at the top of the stairs where I would then check the office to my right and then enter our conference room to my left. I would then walk through the conference room back to another exit near the original doorway that I had walked through. That door had closed to 45 degrees since I walked through it originally.

"That door is always opened all the way and it's a heavy door, so I know I didn't create enough draft walking through for it to close like that. I opened the door back all the way to see if it would move on its own. I even took steps back through my original path to see if a loose floor board maybe caused some movement. Nothing. I've done the same walk-through a hundred times or more, but that door only moved on that one occasion."

One has only to walk inside the SunTrust bank and see the gorgeous restoration to know why it must be tempting for former family residents to come back for a visit. Perhaps the architects did too good a job, making passed-away spirits believe that the house is frozen in time.

Undated photo of the Stephen Upson House
Photo courtesy of SunTrust Bank

The Stephen Upson House

SunTrust Bank
References

Waters, John C. "Upson House: A Link From the Past to the Future." *Athens Tempo*. SunTrust Bank Historical Binder

Miscellaneous clippings in the SunTrust Bank Historical Binder

Author interview with SunTrust Bank Teller Coordinator Derrick Allen

BERNSTEIN FUNERAL HOME

In 1911, Mose Bernstein founded Bernstein Funeral Home and Cremation Service on Broad Street in Athens. Bernstein not only provided funeral services for members of the Athens community, he was an entrepreneur and inventor as well. He developed the first motorized hearse in the state of Georgia, built on a 1913 Ford chassis. He also went on to produce the first factory-assembled hearse.

At that time, family members in a funeral procession typically rode to the gravesite behind the hearse in a horse-drawn carriage. Since most of the roads in Athens were dirt roads, this made for a very dusty ride. Bernstein had the idea to provide a water wagon that rode ahead of the funeral procession to wet the road, which kept the dust to a minimum during the ride.

Bernstein expanded his operations to run several undertaking parlors in nearby communities. He also offered a "burial insurance society" service that patrons could use to prepay funeral services.

After running the funeral home for decades, Bernstein passed away in 1948. Never having children, he left no descendants, so his wife turned the business over to his five employees, allowing operations to continue.

Bernstein Funeral Home still operates today, but moved out of the Broad Street location back in 1970. When they moved, they left behind a wealth of stories about the historic downtown building they occupied for decades, processing the bodies of the deceased.

The building at 424 East Broad Street is now owned by the University of Georgia and is known as the Business Services Building.

Carol Bishop spoke with an employee of Bernstein's who was familiar with tales of the original downtown location. "There is a weird service elevator in there that is always kept locked," Bishop told me. "That elevator was used to carry bodies from the basement where the embalming room was once located up to the funeral parlor for services."

This elevator is kept locked, in part, due to strange moans and other unexplained sounds that often come from the basement. Some employees chalk up these sounds to the settling of the historic building, but some aren't so sure. This may be because not only are unusual sounds reported in the basement, but smells as well.

In the early 20th century, a band of Gypsies reportedly came through Athens every few years. One of these stops in Athens turned tragic as a baby girl in the group died. Her parents left the little girl's body at the funeral home and promised to return for her after they had enough money to pay for the funeral. Sadly, they never returned and the baby girl's body stayed at the funeral home for 50 years.

In the end, the Bernstein family buried the little girl's body in the Oconee Hill Cemetery. They also bought a large spray of red roses, which they placed on her grave.

In years since, people have reported a strong smell of roses in the basement and in other parts of the building. "They say you can still smell the roses from her ceremony in the embalming chamber," Bishop told me.

Some theorize that the moans are piteous cries from the abandoned Gypsy girl and the scent of roses is a reminder of her time here on Earth. Perhaps these events are signs of the parents' long overdue return and attempt to make amends for abandoning their child. The only ones who know for sure are the brave souls that unlock the spooky elevator and venture down into the unknown.

Bernstein Funeral Home
References

"Bernstein Funeral Home and Cremation Services." History. Dignity Memorial. Web. 09 Sept. 2016. <http://www.dignitymemorial.com/bernstein-funeral-home/en-us/history.page>.

Bishop, Carol. "Haunted North Campus Walking Tour Script". Athens-Clarke Heritage Foundation tour on July 20, 2010.

Morales, Kristen. "Bernstein Celebrates 100 Years of Helping Families through Grief." Online Athens. *Athens Banner-Herald*, 16 Oct. 2011. Web. 09 Sept. 2016.

Author interview with Carol Bishop, Librarian for the University Archives at the University of Georgia

AROUND ATHENS AND NEARBY NEIGHBORHOODS

ATHENS-BEN EPPS AIRPORT

Benjamin Thomas Epps was the first Georgian to build and fly an airplane. The electrical contractor, mechanic, and inventor was born on February 20, 1888 in Oconee County. In 1905, the imaginative Ben Epps had already begun designing aircrafts.

After a brief stint at the Georgia Institute of Technology in Atlanta, Ben Epps came home to Athens where he started a bicycle and auto repair shop in 1907. At this shop on Washington Street in downtown Athens, Ben devised designs for airplanes, much like his contemporaries, the Wright brothers, who also built and repaired bicycles and airplanes. Epps used his mother's sewing machine on fabric for the wings of his aircraft.

In 1908, when Ben was just nineteen years old, his first plane took flight, traveling about 100 yards at an altitude of 50 feet. This has been memorialized by Mr. Todd of Winterville, Georgia, as related below:

> In 1907, [Epps] was photographed outside his shop with the first plane he had completed. Mr. Marion N. Todd of Route 1, Winterville, Georgia, remembered seeing Mr. Epps

fly his aircraft around 1908. Mr. T. W. Reed, an Athens editor and historian, wrote about Mr. Epps' first flight in his flying machine in his column, "Echoes from Memoryland," in the Athens Banner in 1946. Mr. Reed was an eye witness to the event. According to Mr. Reed, the first attempt to get the machine off the ground and into the air failed, but the second attempt was successful. The plane got up about 40 or 50 feet and maintained its flight about 100 yards. Then it came down and as it hit the ground it lost both wings, but fortunately pilot Epps was not even scratched.

Later, striving to make air transport available to the masses, Ben Epps created what he called a light monoplane, which was a single-seat aircraft. He designed his plane using bicycle wheels and a buggy seat so the pilot sat upright. He also made use of a hill as a runway. This differed from the approach used by the Wright brothers, who used a takeoff rail and positioned the pilot prone on one wing.

In August of 1909, Mr. Epps launched his second craft, which reportedly became airborne briefly before crashing and being destroyed.

In 1919, Ben partnered with friend and aviator L. Monte Rolfe to create the Rolfe-Epps Flying Service which taught Georgia's first pilots in addition to offering passenger flights and aerial photography services. Epps rented land three miles outside Athens for Epps Flying Field, which was Georgia's first civilian airport. To this day, Athens-Ben Epps Airport remains in the same location and is named for the famed aviator.

Epps shared his love of flying with his children. In 1929, at age thirteen, Ben Epps, Jr. became the youngest pilot ever to fly solo, which garnered so much attention he was invited to the White House to visit President Herbert Hoover. The father and son traveled across Georgia stunt flying and starring in air races.

Ben Epps, Sr., was sadly killed in Athens in 1937 during takeoff for the test flight of a new airplane design.

At the Athens-Ben Epps Airport, some employees believe that the spirit of Ben Epps watches over the hangar and runways to be sure that everyone flies safely. Others believe it could be the ghost of a World War II pilot who spent time there working on planes, but then died in the theater of war and came back to visit.

More than a decade ago, an airport employee was working in a hangar by himself late at night. "At least, he thought he was there by himself," related Mrs. R., a researcher.

"He was in a hangar cleaning the cockpit of a small plane when he heard footsteps approaching the aircraft across the cement floor. He thought the person he heard was his supervisor, so he called out, 'Hey, I'm in here.' He got no response."

Next, he heard a door to the craft open. The door was located behind the wing of the aircraft. The employee walked toward the back of the craft to greet whoever it was. "You can imagine his surprise when he walked back there and found that the door was still shut and no one was inside."

Puzzled, the employee returned to the cockpit and resumed cleaning. It wasn't long before he heard footsteps approaching the plane a second time. He grabbed a flashlight, returned to the back of the plane, and waited. Again, he heard the door open. He flashed the light at the door as soon as he heard it. Again, the door was closed and no one was there.

The employee spun around and returned to the cockpit. He gathered his things and went right home.

According to Mrs. R., "The experience really freaked him out. He swore he was never going to work there at night again."

Athens-Ben Epps Airport References

Hudson, Paul S. "Ben Epps (1888-1937)." New Georgia Encyclopedia. 01 November 2013. Web. 25 July 2016.

"History of Ben Epps." Athens-Clarke County, GA - Official Website. Athens-Clarke County, GA. Web. 09 Sept. 2016. <http://athensclarkecounty.com/1019/History-of-Ben-Epps>.

Author interview with a local researcher for the Athens-Clarke Heritage Foundation.

LADY OF THE BLUE VEIL

The home at 340 Boulevard where Jack Thomas lived was first known for being bright pink. Jack and his father were antiques dealers and the colorful house was filled with a collection curated over decades. One particular antique piece made the house famous for more than its unusual color.

In May of 1965, Thomas acquired a bust of a Gypsy girl from his sister. Afterward, the Thomas household contained one additional member. Thomas' experiences were described in the article "Shadows of the past inhabit the homes of Athens" by Doug Matyka:

> It all began back in 1965 with the sale of the Phinizy family estate, at which Jack's sister purchased a bust depicting the head of a young, shawl-draped woman with very attractive features. Although members of the Phinizy family remember seeing the bust in the home, no one seems to know for sure just where it came from. Speculation has it, however, that the elder Phinizy, who built and sold wagons and carriages, may have received it in trade from a band of gypsies which used to make regular stops

in Athens, primarily for the purpose of burying their dead in Oconee Hills Cemetery.

Whatever the case, shortly after the bust was purchased by Jack's sister, strange things began happening in her home. One daughter who said she had seen a ghost which looked exactly like the bust of the young lady left home, vowing not to return until the bust — and the ghost — were gone.

Valerie Ready's 1983 article "Restless Spirits," detailed Jack Thomas' experiences:

> Thomas had to pry an explanation out of his sister to find out why she was so eager to get rid of the bust. And when he found out why, "I laughed all day because to me, at least at that time, there was no such thing as a ghost. Then two days later, I saw her. I was sitting in the kitchen drinking a cup of coffee. I looked up and saw her standing in the doorway. I thought I was losing my mind. I looked back at my coffee and looked up again and she was gone. At first, I thought I was hallucinating. But, then one day, our little dog saw her at the same time I saw her and she ran at her and started barking and growling. The ghost disappeared and our dog went under all the furniture looking for her. It was then that I knew it hadn't been my imagination. I knew she was a real thing."
>
> One afternoon later as he came up his driveway, the young lady was waiting for him on the porch, and although Jack couldn't see her face, he immediately recognized her clothing as that of the woman in the bust. When he got out of his car and tried to approach her, she did as any good ghost would and disappeared. After that day, however, she was waiting for Jack every afternoon when he came home and he became accustomed to seeing the apparition. (Matyka)

> "When I see our ghost, she's a complete personification. I mean, you can't see through her." Thomas explained. She is always wearing a veil and long dresses down to her ankles. She wears old-time shoes that look as if they may be high-tops. "Ever since then, she's had the run of the house. Every day when I came in from work she would show up on the side porch. She never bothers anything. Sometimes she goes out on the porch and sits in the swing." (Ready)

The Conoly Hester article "Charles Kuralt Is Enjoying Road Life" details more:

> Thomas further specified that the ghost was 5 feet tall, around 100 to 110 pounds, and is solid, not a wispy figure. Surprisingly, the ghost appears to change clothes, alternating between three dresses that are the same style, but different colors. "No one has ever seen her face," he said. "She always wears a shawl over her head." The ghost appears more during daytime hours than at night. "She shows at odd times," Thomas says. "Sometimes she sits in a rocking chair on the front porch in the daytime. Only trouble is, when she goes back in the house, she doesn't use the door." Thomas believed that the spirit liked his house because it was filled with things from her time, such as Victorian furniture and Thomas' large collection of antique dolls. According to Thomas, the bust itself "changes her expression from time to time and her eyes move."
>
> Quite naturally, others to whom Jack told the story of his ghost were skeptical and many made fun of the idea. But, as time passed various friends of Jack's also experienced the presence of the young lady. One man driving down Boulevard saw the woman on Jack's front porch clad in her long, old-fashioned dress. As he later related the story to Jack, the sight of the woman sent chills

down his back and he exclaimed, "If I hadn't known your house was on down the street. I would have thought I was seeing your ghost". After Jack had asked the friend to describe the woman and the house where she had been, he informed the friend that it had been his home and it was indeed his ghost! And another believer in ghosts was made on the spot. (Matyka)

Thomas' neighbors have grown accustomed to the ghost, he said. "The people who have seen her say that she never opens the front door. She just fades through it and disappears. People get a big kick out of it." (Ready)

One of the nicest things about his ghost, according to Jack, is the fact that she brings good luck to those who see her. On more than one occasion, after an appearance by the ghost Jack has found large sums of money or other valuables, none of which anyone ever claimed. And, he says others who have seen her have also experienced good fortune. Now, many people who drop by to visit can't leave before patting the bust for good luck. There are of course many skeptics who refuse to believe that such a thing as a ghost exists at all and they regard stories of their presence as yarns designed to scare children and amuse adults. But, for the Jack Thomases, at least, the existence of spiritual beings is an accepted fact. Jack is always ready to talk about his ghost and even speaks before interested groups about her. And, he never worries about what others think about a grown man who believes ghosts. "People call me crazy." he says. "but as long as my wife calls me at suppertime. I don't mind." He is satisfied and has been for the last five years, to share his home with the ethereal young woman who has changed his life. (Matyka)

She's a well-known ghost who has been written up in the newspapers and discussed on radio and television. Charles Kuralt visited to film an episode of "On the Road" about her. Thomas said the CBS news correspondent sat around his house for six hours hoping to see the ghost. After he left, Thomas found out one of Kuralt's cameramen did see her. "He didn't tell me about it. I heard about it on TV." Thomas believes some people are more sensitive to ghosts than others. "We had a Frenchman come here one time. He would break out in goosebumps and this was in July. He would walk into one room of the house and start shivering and his teeth would start chattering. He was very sensitive to the ghost. Thomas refuses to let anyone bother his ghost. He wants to make sure she feels comfortable and welcome in his home. "We don't want her disturbed. She's calm. She's peaceful. She likes it here and she is welcome here. We've had a lot of fun with our ghost." (Ready)

University of Georgia Hargrett Special Collections librarian Carol Bishop lived near Jack Thomas' pink house growing up. "My father was a friend of his father's."

"People driving by claimed to see the gypsy woman standing on the porch," Carol told me. "When I was a kid, it was a big thing to do, to drive by the house and see if you could see her standing on the porch. And, supposedly, whenever you saw her, you'd come into some money. She was a good ghost."

Jack Thomas remembers a time when he didn't believe in ghosts and says he is glad he found out otherwise. "I never believed in ghosts. I always thought it was a figment of the imagination. I found out later—to my pleasure, I might add—that ghosts are quite real. I don't doubt anymore that there are restless spirits roaming this world, and Athens has an abundance." When asked if he would like to come back as a ghost, Thomas smiled slowly and nodded his head. There is no doubt in Thomas' mind about where he would want to stay if he could come back as a ghost. "Right here. We love this old house. "Thomas said his return to the pink house would be appropriate. "I always tell my friends, I was born on the Boulevard and I have come back to die on the Boulevard." (Ready)

Some claim that the bust of the Lady of the Blue Veil remains in the house on Boulevard to this day. If you pass by and see her ghost rocking on the front porch, you will know for sure.

Lady of the Blue Veil
References

Coffee, Hoyt. "Spirits still roam Athens." *The Red and Black*. October 28, 1983. (Clipping from the Georgia Ghosts folder in the Hargrett Library collection.)

Hester, Conoly. "Charles Kuralt Is Enjoying Road Life." *Athens Banner-Herald*. November 30, 1979. (Clipping from the Georgia Ghosts folder in the Hargrett Library collection.)

Matyka, Doug. "Shadows of the past inhabit the homes of Athens". (Undated and unidentified clipping from the Georgia Ghosts folder in the Hargrett Library collection.)

Morgan, Terry. "Athens has its share of ghastly ghouls and Halloween horrors." *The Red and Black*. (Undated clipping from the Georgia Ghosts folder in the Hargrett Library collection.)

Ready, Valerie. "Restless Spirits" *Athens Banner-Herald*. September 1983. (Clipping from the Georgia Ghosts folder in the Hargrett Library collection.)

Author interview with Carol Bishop, Librarian for the University Archives at the University of Georgia

THE HOUSE ON GLENHAVEN AVENUE

The Cobbham Historic District is one of Athens oldest, and arguably, most beautiful neighborhoods. Originally, the area was outside of town and considered rural, making it one Athens' earliest suburbs. Situated northwest of downtown, the Cobbham neighborhood today remains residential for the most part. Stunning historic homes still grace shaded, tree-lined streets.

Prior to the Civil War, stately home sites in Cobbham sometimes covered entire blocks, including gardens and pastures. After the war, Victorian houses sprouted between the antebellum homes. In 1834, property owner John A. Cobbham subdivided a large tract of farmland and advertised 80 lots for sale.

Though it looks to be from the early 1900s, records for one Cobbham home do not specify when the house was originally built. The earliest sale showing in public records is dated 1979. A classic two-story four-square, the Glenhaven Avenue residence boasts two covered porches and a tremendous, ancient oak tree that may have been planted when the home was built.

In 2003, the home was renovated and converted into a duplex. During this process, the entire inside was gutted to create two one-bedroom apartments, one in the front half of the house and one in the back. Each apartment was two stories tall with stairs up to a loft bedroom.

When the upstairs of the house was gutted, the floor was completely removed from one room of the four-square to allow a 20-foot ceiling in the living room below. Combined with wall-to-wall windows in the living room, the apartment was exceptionally open and airy. The front apartment looked over the street and front yard. A narrow driveway ran close to the house toward the back yard and common parking area.

An Athens resident moved into one of the apartments shortly after it was remodeled. "I loved the apartment. It was beautiful," they assured me. "But, after a while, I realized there was something strange going on there."

"Something strange happened several times before I noticed a pattern to this strange event. I would be awakened very early in the morning by a conversation in low tones. It kind of sounded like people were standing in the driveway right next to the house talking, but trying to be quiet. I couldn't make out what they were saying, just two voices in low tones. The first one or two times it happened I rolled over and ignored it. I thought someone from the front apartment was walking down the driveway to their car or coming from their car to the apartment, although I never heard a car, just the low voices.

"After being awakened a few times and growing curious about who it was and what they were doing there, I would try to catch them when the voices awakened me, since it was a loft bedroom and I could just roll out of bed and look over the loft wall. The huge wall of two-story windows around the living room looked out over the driveway, and another row looked out over the back yard and parking area. If someone had been in the driveway or parking area and close enough for me to hear them talk in a low voice, I should have been able to see them. But, I never could.

"I would hear them and it would pull me out of a deep sleep and I would jump out of bed as fast as I could and look over the wall, across the living room and through the wall of windows. No one would be in the driveway, no one would be out back. And yet, I could still hear the low tones of someone talking. I got the impression it was one person talking to another, but I couldn't tell for sure if it was more than one voice. And, I certainly never saw anyone.

"After so many times of trying to catch sight of them, and failing, it dawned on me what was likely going on. The voices were not coming from outside the house at all, they were coming from inside. When I looked out across the open living room area, the voices were actually coming from the area that used to be a room on the second floor, where they had removed the floor during the remodel. I was probably just a few feet away and staring right at them, unseeing.

"I wonder if they laughed to see me lunge out of bed and try in vain to see who it was talking. At least, I never heard them laughing."

The invisible low-talkers were not the only creepy event that plagued this resident in the loft.

"One night, as I lay in bed, I began to hear noises like a radio, even though no radio was on. In fact, there wasn't even a radio in the house then. But still, I would hear sounds like an old-fashioned radio that you had to turn the knob to tune it. It sounded like someone was flipping through the dial trying to find a station. You would get a flash of music and then static and then a bit of a conversation and then more static. I never heard a whole song or conversation though. It was loud enough to be distinctive and it was driving me crazy since I was trying to go to bed.

"I sat up to try to figure out where it was coming from. But, when I sat up, I couldn't hear it anymore. So, I laid back down. Then, I would hear it again. I realized the radio sound seemed to be coming from the pillow. That was pretty freaky!

"And, as if that wasn't bad enough, I lay there listening to the radio noises in the pillow and wondered what the heck was going on. Finally, there was a brief silence with no static or noise. Then, I suddenly heard a voice that very loudly and very clearly said my name.

"I sat bolt upright in that bed with wide eyes. After that night, I had no more doubts that, for some reason, the veil was indeed very thin at this location."

This tale serves to remind this that, even though a place may be remodeled to look lovely and new, spirits from the past may remain to carry on as if nothing has changed. You never know when it might be prudent to sleep with one eye open, just in case.

The House on Glenhaven Avenue
References

Sheftall, John. "History." Historic Cobbham Foundation. Historiccobbhamfoundation.org, 12 June 2016. Web. 09 Sept. 2016. <http://www.historiccobbhamfoundation.org/history-2/>.

Author interview with a local Athenian

THE HOUSE ON MILLEDGE CIRCLE

In the early 1970s, Athenian Don Nelson moved into an innocuous house located at 190 Milledge Circle. Or, at least, it seemed harmless at the time.

Even after years as a seasoned journalist in the Athens area, Mr. Nelson vividly remembers the strange events that took place in the house long ago.

"We just called it '190,'" Nelson told me. The house is on the corner of Castalia and Milledge Circle, down from where the Five Points Fire Hall is now.

Shortly after moving in, Nelson and his roommates discovered something unsettling. "We found that a door in a hallway that led down to the basement," Nelson began. "So, we went down to check it out. When we got down there, there was a witch's pentangle (pentagram) painted on the floor of the anteroom of this basement area. We thought that was kind of strange.

"We had heard from the neighbors that at one time there were several young college girls who lived there, and thought maybe they had a witches' coven or something. There were rumors one of the girls committed suicide. But, all of that was speculation."

They also found an old barrel filled with dirt and newspapers that dated back to the 1940s. It was an inauspicious start to a decidedly creepy stay in the home.

"My first experience in the house was one day in the early afternoon when I was home alone," Nelson began. "We always left the door open because people came and went all the time. Now, the front door to the house had a particular sound. When somebody came through the front door, you could hear it and you knew that it was the front door opening and the front door closing.

"I was washing dishes in the kitchen, which was at the back of the house. There was a living room and a dining room and a hallway off from those, so there were a couple of ways to access the back of the house.

"At the time, no one was home with me and as I washed dishes. Then, I heard someone come in the front door. I kept washing dishes expecting someone to walk back or call out, but I didn't hear anything.

"I wondered about it, so I stopped washing and walked up front and looked around. The front door was closed.

"I called out, 'Hey—who's here?' Nothing.

"So, I walked back to the kitchen and start washing dishes again. A few minutes later, I hear the door open and close again.

"So, I stop, go up, look around, and there's nobody there. It was kind of strange at that point. I thought 'Well, maybe I'm just imagining things.'

"A few minutes later, I start back washing dishes. And it happens again! Except this time, it was faster. It wasn't like someone just casually coming in the door and closing it, it was like they were hurrying.

"I immediately go running up and there's nobody there.

"Now, I'm getting kind of antsy. I go back to washing dishes. Then, I hear the front door open and slam shut, and then the sound of a person running down the hallway. The footsteps approached and at the point when they would run through the kitchen, I turned towards the doorway. I didn't see anything, but I loudly yelled, 'BAH!'

"That was the end of it. By that last time, the hairs on the back of my neck were raised. It really got me on edge. I swore I heard something coming down that hallway. At the time it should have appeared, it just took my breath away.

"The doorway to the basement was also in the same hallway where the phantom footsteps originated.

"That door opened so that it swung into the basement over the stairs. It was a hazard, so we were always very careful to keep that door closed and keep it latched," Nelson told me. "And, particularly, if we had people over, we would latch it to be safe.

"One night we were having a party in the house. We were all upstairs. I was standing in the hallway with two other guys and one lady. We were standing by the door to the basement talking when she leaned back on the door. That door popped wide open and she just tumbled down the stairs.

"Fortunately, she didn't fall all the way down the stairs and luckily didn't get hurt. We rushed down after her and brought her back up. For the life of us, we can't figure out why that latch was undone. That was something we were always conscious about because it was such a danger.

"I remember it distinctly because I'm so thankful that she wasn't hurt."

Nelson was not the only tenant disturbed by unseen visitors to the house. One of his roommates had more than one unsettling experience.

"One roommate lived in a bedroom towards the front of the house. He told us he woke up at night hearing a baby cry.

"He thought it was coming from his closet. He would get up and check out the closet, but there was nothing there. This happened to him several times."

The spooks were also not afraid to harass multiple people in the home at one time.

"Once, there were two or three of us there when we heard strange sounds coming from beneath the house.

"First we heard several banging noises and then this real weird sound. I'm still trying to convince myself that it was a cat that had gotten caught somewhere up under the house, but I don't see how it could have gotten into the heating system down there.

"It was so strange. We went out and checked all over and checked the basement, but we couldn't find anything."

The House on Milledge Circle
References

Head, Matthew. "Ghosts of Athens, GA (Long but Good!)." *Google Groups*. Newsgroup post. 3 May 1999.

Author interview with Don Nelson

THE POPE ON PRINCE

The Pope on Prince is an eclectic vintage goods shop. Until recently, it was located at 523½ Prince Avenue in Athens. Perhaps the "half" designated in its address is indicative of its tendency to cross between this world and the next.

Owner Monica Bischoff is originally from Nicaragua and opened Pope on Prince two years ago to serve the needs of the many vintage fans in the Athens area.

"It is a beautiful building," Monica told me. Originally, she rented the building to be her apartment. "At first, I had a townhouse downtown. But, this building had everything I really needed. I live here now."

Back when Monica and her daughter were getting the store ready to open, some strange events puzzled them.

"As we were putting things on the walls and getting ready for the grand opening, we were having a lot of issues. The walls have the picture rail molding around the top. Instead of hanging pictures, we decided to use that to hang clothing to display. But, when we hung up dresses, they would drop off. Nothing we were hanging was too heavy, but we would find them on the floor.

"At first, we didn't think anything of it. But later, I got the idea that, maybe, rather than the building, it is the clothing, because they are vintage pieces. After I stopped trying to hang those particular dresses, I stopped having any incidents."

Wayward clothing was not the only trouble they ran into setting up the store. Trying to be social-media savvy, they wanted to create a Facebook page for the store. Apparently, some previous tenants took the opportunity to photo bomb.

"My daughter was taking pictures of the store for our Facebook page. After taking a bunch of pictures, she said 'I don't know what the problem is. I keep getting this...stuff. I can't figure out which one of the lights is causing it.' All the pictures taken in the front room had about 15 orbs. This was the area where we'd had trouble hanging the dresses."

Orbs are a light anomaly appearing in photographs that some people believe are proof of spirit presence or activity.

"After that, I haven't dared to take pictures in the rest of the building. Certainly not at night."

"We put it to the back of our minds. We had a business to open! One day, weeks later, my husband and I were in the front room, where the orbs had appeared in the photos. This was on the second floor of the building and he and I were setting up some displays.

"We have a granddaughter that is four years old. Out of the corner of our eye, both my husband and myself saw a small child run across the room and out the window. The balcony outside the window is high off the ground, but the railing is ridiculously low. Like, a foot and a half."

"Both my husband and I immediately ran out, screaming our

granddaughter's name, 'Wren! Wren!' When I did not see her out on the balcony, my heart just sank. I leaned over the railing and looked down. But, she wasn't there."

Monica and her husband went in the back of the building to the apartment. There they found Wren, safe and sound. "We both thought it was so weird that we both saw a little kid run by. Again, we brushed it off as some kind of trick of the eyes. About it being a ghost, my husband said, 'At least it's a kid,' but, I told him, there's something creepy about a little kid ghost."

For a while Monica employed a cleaning lady named Goza. "Her name means 'Joy,'" Monica told me. Goza would come in and clean before Monica would open the store.

"One day, Goza said to me 'You know, Monica, I really love working for you, but I don't think I can come work in the store before you get in. The other day, I was cleaning and this child was playing behind me. I assumed it was Wren. But, when I turned and looked, there was no one there. I thought maybe you were both in the store, in the back. But, when I went in the back, no one was there.'"

Monica did not pretend to be surprised to hear this story. According to Goza, it was a regular occurrence. "This has happened several times," she told Monica. "It's just too scary for me."

"Then, things continued to get weirder!" Monica exclaimed.

"I had a regular customer who used to work in the planning department for the city of Athens. He was in the store and something happened. I have never seen anything like it. A sure poltergeist."

Monica explained to me that a group of books had been displayed in such a way that one book was placed in front of another book in front of another book. The book that was closest to the wall was the highest because they were sitting on little stairs. In order to get the last book, you literally had to pull it straight up very carefully, because otherwise you would knock down the rest of the displayed books.

As the man shopped near the display, a book came flying out of the cabinet.

"It's a really, very heavy book," Monica explained. "It just came flying over all the books in front of it. None of the other books were moved. It flew at least four or five feet across and almost hit him.

"After it happened, the customer looked at me and said, 'What the hell was that?!' I said, 'I don't know. We have stuff like this happening all the time.'"

"He doesn't come to the store much anymore," she admitted. "It scared him really badly."

Another day, a customer came into the store and informed Monica that, during the 1980s, he had worked to restore the walls in the building. At that time, the person who purchased the building spent almost two years completely remodeling it. He told Monica that the building was rumored to have been the headquarters for the Ku Klux Klan in the area long ago.

"The man said that some interesting things happened in here when they were working on the walls," Monica told me. But, he did not elaborate on the specifics of events.

Monica has made up her mind about the paranormal activity in her shop. "If you ask me, 'Is the building haunted?' I can tell you I've had customers literally run out of the building screaming. They don't stop to tell me 'Bye' or why they are running and screaming. They're just obviously very disturbed."

"So, if you ask me, 'Is the building haunted?' then, I'm gonna tell you 'Definitely, YES! Why? I don't know."

She is sure about one thing. Being in the store in broad daylight is much different than being there after sundown. "Something happens after dark," she confided. "It's a pretty interesting change. The whole building changes at night.

"Several of the college girls that have worked here tell me they do not like to be here after dark because it feels really weird. I even had to cut the store hours because of this. Before, I used to be open a little bit later."

"In Nicaragua, where I am from, we have a very close relationship with the spirit world," Monica explained. "It's part of life. In my country, we say that the day is for the living and the night is for the dead. As a culture, we pay respect by not working late into the night. Because you are disturbing the 'neighbors.'

"As far as the stuff that happens in this building, I look at it like I am just sharing this space. I'm going to make it as harmonious as I can for me and for whoever else is here."

THE POPE HAS RELOCATED TO DOWNTOWN ATHENS AT 119 JACKSON STREET.

The Pope on Prince References

Author interview with Monica Bischoff

CHAPPELLE GALLERY

The Haygood House was built in downtown Watkinsville, Georgia, for Superior Court Judge Joseph Ligon in 1827. In 1839, Ligon sold the house and 17.5 acres to his good friend, Watkinsville attorney Green Haygood.

Green Haygood and his wife, Martha, lived in the house where six children were born. Unfortunately, two of the children, Pitt and Amelia, died in the house just after their first birthdays and are buried on the Haygood House property.

Oldest child Atticus grew up to become an editor, author, and educator. He was a Bishop of the Methodist Episcopal Church and chaplain to the Confederate army during the Civil War from 1861 to 1865. He served as president of Emory College in Oxford from 1875 to 1884.

Fourth child Laura Haygood was admitted to Wesleyan College at age fifteen. After graduating two years later in 1864, she founded a school for girls. At age forty, she became the first female sent into foreign missionary work in China by the Women's Missionary Society of the Methodist Church. Laura died in 1900 and is buried in Shanghai.

In 1926, Haygood Memorial United Methodist Church was founded in Atlanta in honor of Laura Haygood and her brother Bishop Atticus Green Haygood.

Laura's brother Willie became an attorney and sister Myra married and raised a family.

On the Haygood House property, the graves of the two infant Haygood children were unnerving from the beginning. As a child, Atticus would not play near the big tree beside the graves, even going so far as to walk around it as he walked to retrieve mail from the mailbox.

For a while, the house was a church parsonage. When the church sold the property in the 1970s, the headstones were moved from the children's graves to the front of the house where a historical marker was placed to indicate the history of the Haygood family. Sadly, the actual graves remained further back near the driveway and are no longer marked.

In 1914, the Haygood House was renovated to add new kitchen and dining room structures, as well as adding numerous new windows. The number of windows in a home purportedly correlated to a family's wealth.

Kathy and Jerry Chappelle purchased the Haygood House in May of 1999. At that time, some walls were falling inward, several windows needed replacing, and the exterior needed extensive work.

In an interview with the *Athens Banner-Herald*, the Chappelles said, "We're at the stage of our lives where we're looking for a change, a new adventure. It's time to liven up things a bit."

They bought the home with the intention to eventually open the Chappelle Gallery, which would sell pottery and glass art much like their other location, Happy Valley Pottery. They saved the Haygood House from destruction in two ways: from a previous owner in bankruptcy whose fires strayed from the fireplaces and risked burning it to the ground, and from developers who wanted to purchase the land to tear the house down.

I asked Kathy if she had always had an affinity for historic houses.

"In college, I had a boyfriend in Oklahoma and went to visit him one year. I had never seen a Southern historical house before. I thought, 'Boy, I'd like to live in one of those houses someday,' never, ever dreaming that it would come true."

"I heard Haygood House was going to become available and we bought it before it ever went back on the market," Kathy said. "This place was a disaster when we got it. They turned the gas on and immediately turned it back off after they found four gas leaks. At first, we thought we could do the renovation ourselves. But, we realized that was not going to work."

They spent two years renovating and adding 1,600 square feet of living space. "I have been told that the spirits didn't like our addition," Kathy confided.

The entire house was completely rewired, plumbed and insulated. Flooring was installed that was salvaged from the infamous T.K. Hardy Saloon which was in an Athens train station that dated back to the same era as the Haygood House. The wide front porch was restored to close to original.

While the downstairs houses Chappelle Gallery, the upstairs of Haygood House is used as guest quarters or rented out as a Bed and Breakfast. "The nearby Ashford Manor Bed and Breakfast needed a place to recommend for overflow when they were booked up and suggested we could rent out the rooms upstairs. Otherwise, I might never have thought about it."

When they first completed the remodel, an addition included 800 square feet downstairs in the back of the gallery where Kathy and Jerry would live.

But, before they moved in, some friends of her daughter's stayed there a few nights. That was when the spooky experiences began for the Chappelles.

"At night, when they were in bed, they would hear knocking on the door. It didn't even dawn on them that the ghost could go right through."

After Kathy and Jerry moved in, the strange sounds continued. "I have also woken up at night hearing knocking on that door." Kathy rapped on the counter to imitate the noise she heard. "And, I used to see strange shadows."

"I've also woken up because the buzzer here at the front door has gone off. I'll get up and go look, but the door is locked and I don't see anybody outside, there's no cars outside. Everything seems to still be in place."

Kathy believes that the Haygood children are not yet done with their childhood home. "We used to have a lot of noise from 'the kids.' They loved the holidays and would always play with the Christmas balls. I would hear all this noise in the next room from the Christmas balls and think a customer must have come in and I didn't hear it. But, I'd go out there and nobody's there." Another employee would hear the same thing.

In fact, many of the employees at Chappelle Gallery have experienced phenomena they cannot explain.

"When we hired our very first employee, we never said anything to her about the spirits. One day she heard kids clapping and giggling and running up and down the handicapped ramp. She looked out there but didn't see anything. She knew I was in an appointment, so she called Jerry. He could tell by the tone of her voice that she had encountered the spirits. 'Don't worry about it,' he told her, 'They're good. If you're busy, just tell them you're busy.'"

"Later, she was upstairs cleaning the rooms and kept finding the clean towels thrown on the floor." She would pick them up and put them back only to have it happen again.

Another employee was working a shift when he discovered that he was not alone. "He said that he saw someone in all white sitting on top of our pottery display, watching him. That employee ended up not staying too long."

Guests who rent rooms at the Chappelle Gallery have also had their share of run-ins with spooks.

Kathy told me, "One morning, I asked a guest how he slept and he answered, 'I slept pretty good except it felt like someone was tugging the blankets off the bed all night long.' I just said, 'Oh, I'm sorry!' But, he stayed on for another night."

"We had a couple with a baby stay for a couple of months. They would find the baby's toys all over the floor during the night. I suggested they put the toys away and tell the 'other' kids that they could play again in the morning, but now you needed to sleep. That was all that needed to be done. It stopped."

Kathy takes a no-nonsense approach to the spectral visitors. "We had one of the state tourism people here. During the night, he heard a knocking sound at his door. I said, 'If they come knocking at your door, just tell 'em ya gotta go to sleep and they can come back in the morning.' So, he did, and they quit knocking on his door."

Off from a hallway between the two guest rooms upstairs is an area that used to be Atticus' office and is now guest bathrooms.

One guest room is called the Queen Room. A guest who stayed in the Queen Room reported that she kept hearing a crying baby in her room. "She said it sounded like the baby was in the closet." The woman packed up and left in the middle of the night.

Once, a team of paranormal investigators researched the Haygood House and focused on the Queen Room. One team member said there was a soldier named Billy Bob that stayed in the closet. They also described a spirit named Laura, who Kathy thinks could be Laura Haygood. They also described a woman who keeps opening and closing the blinds upstairs and looking out the window towards where the children are buried.

Kathy had her own interaction with Billy Bob. "I was sitting by the door and I asked Billy Bob 'Can you tell us how you were killed in the war?' I immediately got a strong pain in my head, but didn't say so out loud. I asked, 'Were you shot in the head?' Later, one of the team members got in the closet and closed the door. He got the same pain in his head, right in the same spot like I had."

That closet is now used for storage. It sports a large padlock that deters nosy guests, but apparently keeps spirits neither in nor out.

Not everyone that encounters spirits at Haygood House is pleased to do so. Kathy told me, "I had a customer come in, a lady who had lived in Louisiana, in New Orleans. She said, 'You've got spirits in this house and you need to tell them to go home because they are making you sick.' And, I have had a few medical problems. I've asked Billy Bob to go home and asked Laura to go home, but I haven't said anything about the kids yet."

The shenanigans at the Haygood House were not Kathy's first experience with a spooky old house. When they first moved South, prior to owning the Haygood House, Kathy and Jerry purchased the Saxon House in Watkinsville in 1970 and opened Happy Valley Pottery. "Parts of the home were over 100 years old at that time. When we first moved in, it was fall and getting cold, so, I'd close the windows in the boys' room at night. When I would go in the next morning to wake them up, the window would be wide open. This went on for several days. Finally, one day, after the kids were gone to school, I sat down in there and I said 'Now, listen!

We've got to keep these windows closed because I don't want our kids getting sick.' The windows never went back up again."

I asked Kathy what was the most recent activity she could recall in the Haygood House. "There's not so much anymore. A few years ago, we had a guest rent a room who was a preacher from another country. He said he couldn't sleep because of all the spirits in the house. He came down and sat on the steps for about four hours. Without our permission, he was trying to cross the spirits over to where they belonged. Ever since he did that, we hear things once in a while, but not like we used to."

I'm sure Kathy will keep the closet door locked, just in case.

Chappelle Gallery, located at 25 South Main Street in Watkinsville, Georgia, is open 10 a.m. to 5 p.m. and closed on Sundays.

The Haygood House prior to renovations (above)
Photo courtesy of Chappelle Gallery

The Haygood House today (above)
Photo courtesy of Chappelle Gallery

The Queen Room closet where a baby is heard crying

Chappelle Gallery
References

"Haunted Watkinsville." Online Athens. *Athens Banner-Herald*, 25 Oct. 2006. Web. 09 Sept. 2016.

Author interview with Kathy Chappelle

Haygood House history provided by Kathy Chappelle of Chappelle Gallery.

EAGLE TAVERN

The Eagle Tavern in Watkinsville, Georgia, is one of the oldest structures in Oconee County. The tavern has been verified to have existed in 1801, and may have been built even earlier. On the edge of the American frontier, it was built in the area of Fort Edwards.

The Eagle Tavern was originally a four-room structure: two downstairs, two upstairs, plus a basement and cellar. Downstairs was a tavern and general store. It is up for debate if the rooms upstairs were first used as an inn or a family home. Prior to 1860, the area surrounding the tavern was hostile and a tavern in that location would surely have been used as a haven and safe refuge in the event of conflict with Native Americans.

According to local historian Jeff Clarke, the Eagle Tavern was a stagecoach stop and fancy hotel. "It was a tavern and a meeting place because it was on the stagecoach line. The coach arrived three times a week bringing news of the outside world and travelers with money who entertained themselves playing card games. It was an integral part of the community."

On the general store side, stagecoaches pulled right up to the building. The wall on that side has a very tall, very wide door to get barrels and other large items in and out. Ledgers listing customer names and what they bought are still on record in the building. Today, the general store is set up much as it would have been back in the day. Included in the collection are quilts that were made on a functioning loom upstairs in the tavern.

I spoke with Alex Pershka, the Tourism Director for Oconee County who has overseen the Eagle Tavern for the past two years.

"At the time, Watkinsville was the Oconee County seat and the courthouse has always been located across the street from the Eagle Tavern, just as it is today," Alex told me. "Anyone who had official business to do would travel to Watkinsville. It was on the route from Athens to Milledgeville and was the social and political center of the town. Across the street, where the courthouse parking is now, there used to be a park and a well where people would congregate. This was the place to be."

Once the University of Georgia was up and running, a lot of the law students would travel here to study. University founders intentionally placed the campus far from Watkinsville specifically so that students would not be tempted by drinking at the tavern. In fact, if a student got caught on horseback between the University and the tavern, they could be expelled.

Opposite the general store room is the tavern, which includes an original fireplace. The bar itself is as it was originally constructed—in an efficient cubby beneath the stairwell. Clarke County liquor license records show that Robert Richardson took an oath not to sell liquor to slaves or persons of color without permission of their owners or employers in these years: 1849, 1850, 1869, 1870.

The tavern was well known in the area for its food. Records of tavern recipes and menus have survived and show that special meals were served during weeks that court was in session across the street.

Up a set of impossibly steep stairs, the upstairs rooms would have functioned as sleeping quarters.

"The upstairs sleeping quarters were reserved for stagecoach passengers if they wanted to stay the night," Alex said. "It was twelve-and-a-half cents if you wanted to get a spot in the bed. So, if you were traveling, you hoped it was a slow night."

The room displays antique rope-style beds complete with bed keys, which were used to tighten the ropes that held up the mattress if they got saggy. This is where the saying "sleep tight" comes from. Slats were not used in beds until later, and even then, were first used only when the bed functioned as a cooling board for the deceased before a viewing.

In the room situated above the tavern, a cabinet is filled with artifacts found on the property. In this cabinet are portions of large bones. When I asked Alex what kind of bones they were, "I tell people that is from a cow," was his cagey response. Perhaps, a stagecoach traveler met an untimely fate here?

Also on display is the functioning antique loom dating back to the 1840s to 1850s, held together by original wooden dowels.

Artifacts unearthed at the location include the following pieces dating back to the 1800s: five-hole bone buttons, a silver wedding band, a musket ball, musket hammers, gun flints, an 1826 U.S. one cent coin, an 1800 Spanish quarter, bone-handled knives, and brass spectacles.

In the early 1840s, once the railroad was established, it became more cost efficient to travel by train than by stagecoach. It was a little quicker and more comfortable, but not by much. This was the tipping point at which stagecoach use dwindled. After people didn't have reason to stop there, the population in Watkinsville began to decrease.

After it was no longer a tavern, families did reside in the building in the early 1900s.

Over time, twelve rooms had been added to the original four, making the tavern a massive sixteen rooms at its peak with a large front porch.

"Since the additions were done around the original structure, they actually helped insulate and protect the original structure," Alex told me. This aided a restoration project during the 1960s, which removed all but the original four rooms. The tavern walls and ceilings have been replaced but it retains the original wide-plank floors."

In 1958, the Atlanta Journal and Constitution published an interview with Julia Johnston, who lived in the tavern building as a child. She was interviewed in conjunction with the upcoming restoration. Amazingly, Alex ran across a copy of the article when cleaning out a storage room in the courthouse the day after I interviewed him. It included photos and details that had not seen the light of day in decades.

According to the article, Miss Johnston said the following:

> "My great-grandfather, Richard Richardson, bought the place from a Mr. Moon before 1821. My mother and my grandmother and my great-grandmother lived here and ran the Eagle. I'm supposed to live here still, in the new part my great-grandfather added in the 1820s, but the house is in such bad shape. I still remember the old sign that hung outside on a post at the corner. It had a painted eagle with spread wings and the words 'Eagle Hotel' on one side and on the other, 'Accommodations for man and Beast.' I can hear it squeaking now in a high wind.
>
> "Right here on the porch, there always sat a handmade table with a washbowl and bucket on it. Everybody who came in drank from the same dipper. We always had to keep a lid on

the bucket so Mr. Frank Booth's pet crow wouldn't steal the dipper. He took things from all over town and hid them in a hollow tree.

"There was always a skeleton in the cellar when we were children," said Miss Johnston. "The skeleton was that of the first Negro hanged in the county. Dr. Will Richards, who was my grandmother Billups' brother, asked the man if he could have his bones and the Negro told him he could if he'd just give him all the ginger cakes he could eat until the hanging. My mother baked the cakes—she was a little girl then. Dr. Richards kept the skeleton in his office. But he left it here when he moved to Mississippi and it got put in the cellar like everything else. That skeleton was better than burglar bars. They never had to lock the basement doors because nobody would go in the place after dark."

A man was visiting the tavern with a paranormal investigative group when the story about Henry was retold. The man made a sudden connection. The tale of the skeleton rang familiar to an explanation for some bones that had been kept in his family for years. His family was related to the Eagle Tavern doctor and he thought some of his relatives might still have the skeleton.

The hanged man is rumored to be named Henry, or at least, that is how folks refer to him now. They had to give him a name after he started making frequent appearances in the building.

The Oconee County Welcome Center used to be housed in the downstairs of the Eagle Tavern. A local policeman came in to talk to the director of the tavern. After chatting a minute, he asked who was upstairs. She told him no one was upstairs, that she was there by herself.

"No," he said, "as I was coming up the walkway, I looked upstairs and there was a man looking out the window."

"And that's Henry," Jeff Clarke concluded.

"The upstairs sleeping quarters above the general store is the room that Henry looks out of," Alex verified.

"On two different occasions, the Chief of Police was leaving the courthouse across the street and looked up at the Eagle Tavern to see the face of a black male in the upstairs window. Knowing the place should be closed and no one should be in there, he would go in and check it out, but nothing was there."

"We had one volunteer who actually felt a hand on her back when no one was there," Jeff told me. "She quit."

Jeff also volunteers at the Tavern, giving tours in costume and participating in re-enactments. "I was giving a tour down in the cellar for a couple visiting from New York," he continued. "The man asked about ghost stories associated with the tavern and I told him about Henry. Just then, the man felt a hand on his back. Without a word, the man turned around and rushed out of the room. He told me what happened later when we got outside."

Eagle Tavern volunteer Maria Caudill considers herself to be on good terms with Henry and any other spirits who reside there.

"What I always do when I come in the door is yell 'Yoohoo!'" she told me. "I have good feelings about the Eagle Tavern. I've felt a real good presence there. They're my buddies!"

Maria has been a volunteer at the tavern for over six years. Volunteers at the tavern dress in period costumes to give tours and host functions several times a year, such as for student field trips. The volunteers try to maintain an air of authenticity by keeping true to the historic nature of the setting. For example, Maria loves decorating for Christmas using simple greenery and cloth decorations appropriate to the 1800s.

Today, when volunteers enter the tavern, they do not bring any 21st century electronics such as cell phones. Of the atmosphere he has experienced at the Eagle Tavern, Alex says, "I've had nothing but good vibes."

Maria related a story of a strange occurrence from about two years ago. "We were at the tavern after finishing a tour I conducted with Jeff Clarke and another lady for three hundred school kids. We were cleaning up the quilts we had laid down for the children to sit on. After I gathered up the quilts and folded them, I had them piled in my arms. At that time, no one was in the building with me. My arms full of quilts, I was in a jovial mood as I walked up to the back door, realizing it was closed and double-latched. Without really thinking about it, I said, 'Henry, open the door.' And just then, it came right open. I didn't think a thing of it. I just walked on through, then said, 'Thank you, Henry!' And the door closed back."

"It finally dawned on her how weird it was that this big old door just opened in front of her," Jeff added.

Maria's husband has also had a brush with the unexplained in the building. "My husband and I were there on a Saturday morning. Most of the time when we're there doing tours, we're in costume, as we were that day. My husband sat down to wait for me inside the tavern as I stepped out to use the restroom. This is no easy task when you are in costume. When I finally returned to the tavern, my husband was still sitting by one of the stanchions, staring at it. He said, 'As soon as you walked out that door, this chain started swinging back and forth, and back and forth.' He told me that the first thing he did was look outside to the road to check for traffic, but there was none. He told me the chain continued swinging until I approached on the walkway. Then, it stopped."

Jeff Clarke is no stranger to odd experiences at the tavern himself. He told me about an event he cannot explain that happened on a day that the tavern was hosting an event with period-costumed volunteers.

"One Saturday morning, we had set up for some re-enactors to come visit. Some had beautiful antebellum dresses. Another wore a Confederate outfit and knapsack and he described for visitors what a Confederate soldier of that era typically carried. We expected the actors to arrive around 11:00 a.m. I got there about 10:00 a.m. to set up and turn everything on. I went up the ramp to the back door and unlocked it.

"Just inside the door was an alarm panel which I used to turn off the alarm. When I turned away from the alarm panel back to the tavern area, near the front door area was a lady wearing an antebellum era dress. I immediately thought it was one of the re-enactors. She was not ethereal or filmy or smoky or weird at all. It was like looking at you right now. And she was looking back at me.

"She had dark eyes and dark hair that was styled up off her neck. She also wore a ribbon choker around her neck. Her dress was low-cut and scarlet in color. She stood still and watched me. I was a little startled because no one should be in there yet, and I had just turned off the alarm.

"I said to her, 'Hello.' And when I did, she disappeared. She didn't fade away slowly. She was there and then just…boom…gone." Though describing the occurrence as not being ominous, his response was understandable. "I got my ass out of there."

Other volunteers working at the tavern have heard footsteps upstairs walking when no one is in the area. "If you are upstairs, it will be downstairs. If you are downstairs, you hear it upstairs," Jeff says. "It's not like a creak—there's a definite cadence." He thumps has hand on the table in rhythm to replicate the sound. "The sound travels. You can hear the progression across above you or below you.

"And more often than not, it will happen on cloudy days. We would wonder if it was just the house settling. Well, it was built in 1801, how much more settling can it do?"

Rounding out the cast of spiritual characters is a man with a top hat who has been seen downstairs next to the fireplace. Others have reported seeing two little girls.

Schoolchildren on field trips are not the only ones eager to explore the Eagle Tavern. Alex is sometimes contacted by paranormal groups who want to investigate the tavern.

"When investigative groups come, it is hit and miss," Jeff Clarke says. "Sometimes there are cold spots, hot spots and things moving. Sometimes nothing happens. It's a lot like fishing."

One group put tape on the floor in an X to mark a spot and placed a ball on it. They set up cameras focused on the ball and were lucky to catch some unexplained footage. "Around 1:30 a.m., it was ever so slight, but it did move. They checked the area for air vents or windows open, but they found nothing that would explain the motion," Jeff said.

A few groups that have investigated got more than they bargained for.

According to Corinne Underwood in her book *Haunted History: Atlanta and North Georgia*, one welcome center employee described an apparition she witnessed. A dancing lady in a pink dress appeared from thin air. Other employees of the non-smoking facility detected the distinct smell of cherry tobacco while no one was present who smoked. Reportedly, a group outside the tavern witnessed what seemed to be a finger and hand in an upstairs window. But, when the room was examined, no one was present.

During a different investigation, one of the researchers felt a pressure on his lower back as if he were wearing a heavy backpack. When the researchers reviewed their video, it showed what looked like a black figure pressing down on the man's shoulders.

After so many stories being reported, the Eagle Tavern was included as a stop on a local ghost tour. Krista Derbecker's *Red and Black* article describes related experiences:

> Oconee County tourism director Anita Ford and Eagle Tavern Museum's curator Ginny Moon have both had encounters with what psychics claim are five "entities" that dwell in the Tavern.
>
> "We've both smelled tobacco smoke in the doorway. It's so strong we'll go outside to see if someone's out there," Moon said.
>
> Another time, Moon and Ford came back to the Tavern one morning and found that the corn-shuck broom from the downstairs tavern room had been moved to an upstairs room, beside the back window.
>
> They called everyone who might have been in the locked building, but no one said they had moved it.
>
> "That's the honest-to-God truth," Ford said.
>
> To add to the spook factor, the window where the broom was found is the same window where several different people have reported seeing a large black man - when no one is actually in the Tavern, Ford said.
>
> "One guy thought someone had broken into the Tavern," but no one had been in it, Ford said.
>
> The black man is not the only ghost people have claimed to see in the windows.
>
> A few years ago a cleaning lady was across the street in the courthouse one night and noticed a woman dancing and twirling around the room.
>
> "I'm still kind of skeptical, but when I think about what we've seen," Moon said.
>
> "We look for logical explanations but haven't found them yet," Ford added.

One investigative group included Mrs. L., a long time Athens resident and former Eagle Tavern volunteer. She had the distinction of weaving on the antique loom in the tavern during events and tours.

Once, Mrs. L. was about to enter the bedroom across from the loom room when she noticed that the lamp overhead in the bedroom began to sway back and forth on its own.

Mrs. L. had also heard of a young girl who worked at the tavern before her time there. The girl was terrified to go upstairs because she felt like there was something on the stairs.

During one investigation Mrs. L. attended at the tavern, a rocking chair in the front room upstairs began to rock by itself with no one in it or near it. "We all stood around it and watched it rock," she said and indicated that this event was captured on film by the investigators.

During another investigation, Mrs. L. and several other people were sitting upstairs in the room where the loom was. Behind her was the glass case where the tavern stored the artifacts dug up on the tavern property. A boy seated in front of Mrs. L. turned around, looking in her direction.

"He suddenly turned white," she said. "Then, he jumped up and flew down the stairs." Mrs. L. turned to the others and asked, "What's going on?" But, they didn't know.

They all went downstairs. When they found the boy, they asked him what happened. He told them that after he turned around, in the glass case behind where they were sitting, he saw the face of a man.

Mrs. L. said none of the others saw, felt, or noticed anything at the time this happened.

Beneath the tavern is a dirt-floor basement that must be accessed from outside the building. The basement runs the full length of the tavern and is creepy despite currently being kept neat. On one end is a huge original fireplace that was probably used as a summer kitchen when the building was an inn. The other end of the basement was at one time dug out for a cold cellar. Towards the back wall of the basement, there used to be a well that was filled in long ago during renovations.

"Oh, my goodness...there's something in the basement," Mrs. L. confided. "And there's a terrible smell down there they can't get rid of."

She was present when an investigative team checked out the basement. The man and woman set up cameras and recorders to capture evidence. The man also carried a disposable camera in his hand when he entered. After a moment in the darkness, they all heard a strange sound.

"We heard a sound like plastic when it is being crushed, and the man cried out in anguish," Mrs. L. reported. "Then he yelled to both of us, 'We have to get out of here! We have to get out now!' We asked him what happened and why. He said, 'Just go! Just get out!' So we did."

Outside, Mrs. L. examined his hand. Since she was a former emergency room nurse, she saw it was clear he had torn a ligament somehow. He told her that something had squeezed his hand hard enough to tear the ligament and crack the plastic of the camera he was holding. Investigators who reviewed the tapes of the event reported that you could hear the bones crushing on camera.

Mrs. L. told the man that he needed to go get his hand seen to. "He ended up having to have surgery. Can you imagine explaining that when the doctor asked how it happened?"

Later, the same investigative team came back. Again, Mrs. L. again was present during their investigation.

While in the darkened basement, a man on the investigative team used a technique referred to as "provoking." To provoke spirits is to say or do things that you anticipate will anger any spirits present in the hopes that their anger will cause them to react and make their presence known. The men were being antagonizing and spoke into the thick, dark air: "You need to come out and show yourself."

Mrs. L. stood to the right side of one woman on the team. They were so close their shoulders were touching. Suddenly, the woman made a noise and Mrs. L. asked her what was wrong. She replied that she needed to go outside.

Once outside the basement, they examined her neck. It had red scratch marks clawed into it.

Mrs. L. was sure that if the woman had done this to herself that she would have felt her movements since they were right next to each other with shoulders touching.

Sometime later, a different investigative group arrived to study the Eagle Tavern. They braved the terrors of the basement to investigate, but prudently left the lights on.

There was a bench near the back wall of the basement where the well had been filled in. Three men were sitting on the bench.

"I stayed in the background and observed as they conducted their investigation," Mrs. L. reported. The men were using foul language as a provoking technique to taunt whatever spirit might reside in the basement.

Mrs. L. said, "When they called it a coward, I told them, 'Guys I don't think I'd do that if I were you.'" Nonetheless, they continued to provoke. One man on the far left side of the bench was nearest to the corner where the basement walls came together. "From that corner, a gray smoke billowed into the room. As the smoke became more and more solid, the men continued to taunt and provoke the entity, suggesting it was scared of the men. I told them, 'You need to come out of there!' But, they would not be persuaded.

"Suddenly, the man leading the provoking was grabbed by the throat and thrown to his knees by something unseen. He was gasping for air as he was choked. Several team members grabbed the man and dragged him, choking and gagging, out of the basement as the smoke dissipated." After being outside and resting a while, he finally felt better. She said, "I think that's the last time that group came to the Tavern."

Mrs. L. told me that sometime after those events, someone was brought in that was supposed to banish whatever was in the basement. "They scattered herbs and burned sage. They told the tavern employees and volunteers not to move anything for three days, and they did as they were told. But it didn't work. It just didn't work."

Mrs. L. is pragmatic about her experiences at the tavern. "It was pretty interesting at the time. I just don't want to do any of that any more. I wouldn't go back into the Eagle Tavern with anybody. I'm now a Christian. But, those things did happen and there were multiple witnesses. There's no sense me sitting around and trying to say they didn't happen."

TOURS OF THE EAGLE TAVERN MUSEUM ARE AVAILABLE MONDAY THROUGH FRIDAY FROM 10 A.M. TO 4 P.M. CALL 706-769-5197 TO SCHEDULE A TOUR.

Eagle Tavern

The Eagle Tavern in 1836
Photo courtesy of the Hargrett Library collection

The Eagle Tavern in 1937
Photo courtesy of the Eagle Tavern

The Eagle Tavern around 1960, after the restoration
Photo courtesy of the Eagle Tavern

The Eagle Tavern today
Photo courtesy of the Eagle Tavern

Eagle Tavern References

Sparks, Andrew. "Old Eagle Tavern Will Preen Its Feathers Again." *Atlanta Journal & Constitution Magazine*. April 1958. (Clipping supplied by the Eagle Tavern.)

Underwood, Corinna. Haunted History: Atlanta and North Georgia. Atglen, PA: Schiffer Pub., 2008. Print.

Tonge, Jonathan. "Athens Lore on Haunted Tour." *The Red and Black*. The Red and Black, 03 Oct. 2002. Web. 09 Sept. 2016.

Derbecker, Krista. "Spooky Spots Lurk Just around the Bend." *The Red and Black*. The Red and Black, 25 Oct. 2006. Web. 09 Sept. 2016.

"Andy Sparks Papers MS 2777 Eagle Tavern (Watkinsville)." Article from the Hargrett Library collection. Folder 6 of 11.

Author interview with Alex Pershka

Author interview with Maria Caudill

Author interview with Historian Jeff Clarke

Author interview with a long time Athens resident

SMALL SPOOKS

The Barrow-Tate House

In 1879, the Barrow Tate House was a five-room cottage built at 436 Dearing Street by Middleton Pope Barrow. Over time, the house was expanded to fifteen rooms, four baths, and fourteen decorative gables.

Among the members of the Athens community to call the structure home are University of Georgia Chancellor David C. Barrow, Jr., and Dean William Tate.

Tate's descendant, Susan Frances Barrow Tate, lived in the house her entire life. She graduated from the Lucy Cobb Girl's School and the University of Georgia. Tate worked as a librarian for the UGA Special Collections. From her time in the house, several events are still vivid in her memory.

Susan was having a difficult time with a problem, so she lay on her bed with eyes closed and mulled the issue over. After hearing an odd sound, she opened her eyes and saw a man in the doorway.

Nancy Roberts pens Susan's description of the scene in *Georgia Ghosts*:

"I was astonished to see York, a black gentleman who had worked as a yard man for us," she said. "As children, we would walk along with York and ask him questions while he worked. He was always patient with us. York had been dead for many years, yet there he stood, holding his hat in his hands while he looked over at me. He said quite clearly in the kind way he always spoke, 'It's going to be all right, little Missy,' and then he disappeared. And you know, it was all right. I think he came back to keep me from worrying so.

"On another occasion, our dog was lying by the front door. The dog suddenly got up and ran back to the rear of the hall near a door. She paused there, then began walking slowly along, looking up all the time. When she reached the entrance to the parlor, she stared up expectantly. My aunt and her husband were watching this, and she said, 'Whom do you think she sees?' I replied that I didn't know. The dog was now sitting by the fireplace, still looking up expectantly as if into someone's face. My aunt said, 'I know who it is. That must be Papa.'

"At that moment, the dog got up, walked over to my father's empty chair, and stood beside it for a moment as if puzzled. Then, she shook herself and went back to the patch of warm sunlight by the front door where she had been lying before.

"Not long after this incident, a student asked me, 'Mrs. Tate, who is the elderly gentleman who sits on your front porch?' I told her that we didn't have any elderly gentlemen living in the house. 'No one with a beard?' she asked. I replied no again, though I knew she was describing my father who had been dead for years.

Wayne Ford's article "Ghost Hunt" gives this testament by Susan's son, Jeff Tate:

> "My mother, was a very believable, credible person," Tate said. "She is not normally one who would exaggerate," said Tate, whose great-grandfather, David Crenshaw Barrow Jr., was one of the best-known chancellors at the University of Georgia.

Researchers once visited the home to conduct a paranormal investigation. Their devices recorded electronic voice phenomena of laughter and giggling in the attic. In the basement, they also recorded a crying sound that came from a disused stairwell.

The John B. Cobb House

The John B. Cobb House at 575 North Harris Street was once home to John Cobb and his stepdaughter, Mary. When Mary became engaged to Jefferson Lamar, a party was thrown to celebrate the couple's nuptials (though whether this was before the actual ceremony or after is up for debate). Lamar himself was not able to attend the party, as he was in Virginia fighting in the Civil War.

During the celebration, the newly-installed gas lights burned brightly throughout the house. Suddenly, all the lights died out and the house went dark. A family servant quickly lit the fireplaces and distributed candles, saving the party.

It was not until later that Mary and guests of the party found out that on that very night, Jefferson Lamar was killed on a Virginia battlefield. Lamar reportedly died at the very moment when the house had gone dark during the party.

Afterward, some claim Lamar haunted the home, looking for his wife. Others claim Mary haunts the home where she received the tragic news. Still other think the home was haunted by a long-dead family nurse or the servant who re-lit the party.

Regardless of who is responsible, the home reportedly continued to have issues with lighting from that point on.

The Georgian Hotel

The Georgian Hotel opened at 247 East Washington Street in 1909. Atlanta Architect A. Ten Eyck Brown designed the Georgian Revival building that cost $200,000. The state-of-the-art hotel was a landmark for the city of Athens and guests staying there enjoyed modern conveniences such as an electric elevator. The hotel had 100 rooms, each with a private bath and running hot and cold water.

According to historian Jeff Clarke, "The Georgian was one of the premier hotels in the South. Because Atlanta was burned to the ground, Athens was more of a cosmopolitan, metropolitan center."

Tragedy struck at the Georgian in 1912. The children of a hotel guest were playing hide-and-seek in the lobby. After passengers embarked, a careless elevator operator left the brass elevator safety gate open. After the elevator rose, a pit lay exposed in the open elevator shaft.

According to Clarke, "One of the children, a girl named Nyla, got too close and fell down the shaft to her death."

Since that time, the Georgian building has been rumored to have strange goings-on.

"One lady I know that worked as a manager there said that at night, it was one of the most uncomfortable places to be. And one of her associates heard a child giggling when no one else was present," said Clarke.

Other strange reports say "poltergeist-like" activity occurs in the kitchen area, such as pots and pans flying off the wall, doors slamming, and lights flickering.

Currently the Georgian building houses apartments and commercial space.

The Dancers

In a house near Milledge Avenue, on certain Spring days, you can hear music that sounds like piano and violin. This is unusual since there is not a piano in the house and no source for the music can be found. After the music begins, a young couple emerges from a wall and begins to dance. The girl wears a hoop skirt and the boy wears a gray Confederate uniform. They dance for several minutes, then stop by a window. They pause for a moment, then exit through the window as if there used to be a door there. Then, they vanish into thin air.

When the dancers disappear, the piano music stops, at least until their next performance. It is reported this happens up to three times in a month.

The Churchgoer

At one Athens church, a frequent visitor seems to be no longer of this world. In Valerie Ready's article "Restless Spirits," Athenian Jack Thomas reported that he had witnessed the phenomenon.

"There's a church here in Athens. I won't say which one," says Thomas. "There's an old man here with solid white hair who walks up the aisle around twilight. He's real old and wearing an old-fashioned, black worsted suit. I've seen him. He walks down the aisle with an expression on his face you would not believe. It's of complete adoration. He lights the candles and an organ will start to play real low. He walks behind the altar and just vanishes back there."

Delta Tau Delta

Delta Tau Delta member Dave Enichen graduated in May of 2012. In Elizabeth Howard's *Red and Black* article, he described events at the fraternity house at 1084 Prince Avenue.

"It used to be the Kappa Delta house. Back [then,] in the room at the end of the house was a bathroom. A girl was upset with her life. Her boyfriend had broken up with her...and she had hung herself in the bathroom. When we took over the house, we turned it into a bedroom so that it's room six where she would have hung herself.

"The weirdest thing that ever really happened to me was when I was one of the first people to come back after Easter and I was in the house by myself. I was sitting in that room watching Game of Thrones and out of the blue, the surround sound turned on full blast. It shot me out of the couch and I turned it off really quick. Then, as soon as I had sat back down, the surround sound turned back on. I didn't want to turn it back off because I figured she would just turn it back on, so I turned the volume all the way down. It has a little green light that turns on when it's on, so once I had turned the volume all the way down, every once in a while, you would see the little green light go on and off. It was like when I was all by myself, she was really messing with me."

Enichen claims the ghost is friendly and only plays jokes.

UGA Dance Building

Mia Falcon described this story about the Department of Dance building in *The Red and Black* newspaper:

It was 10 a.m. one Friday when Meredith Johnson headed down to the basement of the dance building, innocently stopping by the bathroom before her morning yoga class. Upon entering, Johnson witnessed what appeared to be two young girls, elementary school aged, holding hands and smiling up at her. Johnson hesitated, but continued to a stall without much thought. When she emerged, the small girls were gone, but she never heard them exit.

On the way back upstairs, they passed by her going to opposite direction - back to the bathroom.

"I didn't even hear them leave the bathroom while I was in there, so I have no idea how they got up there so fast," said Johnson, a sophomore engineering major from Milton.

The Mystery House on 78

On Highway 78 heading out of Athens towards Lexington sits a Federal-style residence that has mystified residents for decades. The two-story brick antebellum house dates back to around 1810. Gilbert Head, Archival Associate for the University Archives at the University of Georgia, recalls visiting the home around 1977: "It has been extensively modified and remodeled, but the original one-story core of the house remains intact at the center, including a kitchen and old hand-hewn logs that were part of the fabric of the back walls.

"I noticed there was high wainscoting all through the house and on all of the wainscoting, there were pieces of mirror. The mirrors were placed so that no matter where you were, you had a clear view of all of the entrances, exits and windows in the room. I asked the guy about that and he said, 'Well...we're not here alone. There is a spirit who lives here and we think we see her every once in a while. The manifestations are strongest in the old carriage house.'

"He then related that he had never been able to take a picture where the photograph turned out if the image included the carriage house. He said it always fogged over. We took several pictures on the property that day. In all the pictures we took, any of them that had any portion of the carriage house in it, the photos were fogged over.

"I was at the house for a Halloween event with a friend of mine who claimed an ability for clairvoyance. My friend came out on the back porch and looked like...like he'd seen a ghost! He was so upset, he said he was leaving. Before going, I asked him if he had been drinking and if he was okay to drive. He responded that he had not been drinking, but even if he had, that what happened would have sobered him up. 'I don't want to talk about it.' was all he would say.

"Later, I met a woman who was an elementary school teacher. The Halloween event at the house came up in conversation with her. Surprised, she related that she had lived in that very house. The teacher and her family had lived there for about a year, including a daughter who was about six or seven years old. The girl was described as 'not generally given to flights of fancy.'

"One day the daughter came and asked her mother, 'Is it okay if I go play with my friend Amanda?' Puzzled, her mother responded that since their house was out in the middle of nowhere, she didn't have a friend close by. The child insisted that her friend was there and went on to describe the dress she was wearing. The mother finally relented and said it was okay, as long as she did not go running off.

"Over time, 'Amanda' became the imaginary little friend for the little girl. Months later, the mother was in the attic cleaning and moving things around. Behind a trunk, she found a painting of a seven- or eight-year old girl wearing exactly the dress that her daughter had described. Apparently, it was this Amanda."

Hargrett Rare Book and Manuscript Library

In the late 1950s, the Hargrett Rare Book and Manuscript Library displayed an exhibit about Native American burials that featured an actual ancient skeleton of a Native American. During the month that the display was on exhibit, word began to circulate among employees about strange events taking place in the vicinity of the exhibit. Some said that at night, strange footsteps could be heard around the exhibit area. Janitors voiced their opinion that they were not keen on cleaning anywhere near the case that contained the skeleton.

After the exhibit was taken down and the skeleton was no longer displayed, it was placed in the vault which was located in room 315. During that time period, the department was arranged so that there was a seating area around the outside of the vault where people would study. For unsuspecting patrons who studied at the tables near room 315 during evening hours, a startling surprise awaited them. Many reported hearing strange sounds. Some even reported feeling a cold air blow against the back of their necks.

The reports of disturbances were so numerous that the library decided a change had to be made. They tried to find someone who would return the bones to the Archaeology department, but volunteers for the job were not to be found. Eventually, Director of Special Collections John W. Bonner was forced to take matters into his own hands. He was fed up with complaints from patrons about creepy disturbances and at wits end about the janitors refusing to clean anywhere near the area. His answer to these problems was to personally carry the bones out of the Special Collections library and deposit them at the Archaeology department.

Mr. Bonner's action appeared to have the desired effect. The strange events no longer plagued the area after the bones were removed. Some employees at the library suspect that the ghost left Hargrett for good and followed his bones to wreak havoc across campus wherever his bones traveled. The only thing they were sure of was they were glad the wretched bones were gone.

In the current location of the Hargrett Rare Book and Manuscript Library, a strange presence has been noted in an unusual place: the bathroom.

According to librarian Carol Bishop: "There's something with the women's bathroom. More than one person has sworn there was someone in there, when in fact, no one was in there. It's the first stall. No one uses it. Except the ghost."

Small Spooks References

The Mystery House on 78

Author interview with Gilbert Head, Archival Associate for the University Archives at the University of Georgia

The John B. Cobb House

Head, Matthew. "Ghosts of Athens, GA (Long but Good!)." *Google Groups*. Newsgroup post. 3 May 1999.

Matyka, Doug. "Shadows of the past inhabit the homes of Athens". (Undated and unidentified clipping from the Georgia Ghosts folder in the Hargrett Library collection.)

Author interview with Steven Brown, University Archivist Emeritus

The Georgian Hotel

Clarke, Jeffrey. "Folklore, Facts & Fables Tour"

Athens Downtown Walking Tour. Athens-Clarke Heritage Foundation. http://www.athenswelcomecenter.com/images/downtown_walking_tour.pdf

Author interview with Historian Jeff Clarke

The Dancers

Ready, Valerie. "Restless Spirits" *Athens Banner-Herald*. September 1983. (Clipping from the Georgia Ghosts folder in the Hargrett Library collection.)

Coffee, Hoyt. "Spirits still roam Athens." *The Red and Black*. October 28, 1983. (Clipping from the Georgia Ghosts folder in the Hargrett Library collection.)

The Churchgoer

Ready, Valerie. "Restless Spirits" *Athens Banner-Herald*. September 1983. (Clipping from the Georgia Ghosts folder in the Hargrett Library collection.)

The Barrow-Tate House

Roberts, Nancy. Georgia Ghosts. Winston-Salem N.C.: John F. Blair, 1997. Print.

Head, Matthew. "Ghosts of Athens, GA (Long but Good!)." *Google Groups*. Newsgroup post. 3 May 1999.

Ford, Wayne. "Ghost Hunt." Onlineathens.com. *Athens Banner-Herald*, 31 Oct. 2004. Web.

The Athens-Clarke Heritage Foundation Walking Tour. http://www.athenswelcomecenter.com/images/milledge_ave_walking_tour.pdf

Delta Tau Delta

Howard, Elizabeth. "The Haunted (Greek) Houses of UGA." *The Red and Black*. 05 Sept. 2013. Web. 09 Sept. 2016.

UGA Dance Building

Falcon, Mia. "Hauntings on Campus: Students Share Ghost Sightings and Supernatural Experiences." *The Red and Black*. The Red and Black, 02 Dec. 2015. Web. 09 Sept. 2016.

Hargrett Rare Book and Manuscript Library

Bishop, Carol. "Haunted North Campus Walking Tour Script". Athens-Clarke Heritage Foundation tour on July 20, 2010.

Have you had a spooky experience in the Athens area?

Share your tale at ghostsofathens@gmail.com.

Your story may be considered for inclusion in the next book. No story will be published without the express permission of the storyteller and real names do not need to be used.